EFFECTIVE EXECUTIVE'S

The Eight Steps for Designing, Building, and Managing FrontPage 2000 Web Sites

GUIDE TO FRONTPAGE WEB SITES

EFFECTIVE EXECUTIVE'S

**The Eight Steps for Designing, Building, and Managing
FrontPage 2000 Web Sites**

GUIDE TO FRONTPAGE WEB SITES

Stephen L. Nelson
Jason Gerend

REDMOND
TECHNOLOGY
P R E S S

Effective Executive's Guide to FrontPage Web Sites:
The Eight Steps for Designing, Building, and Managing FrontPage 2000 Web Sites

Copyright © 2000 Stephen L. Nelson and Jason Gerend

Published by
Redmond Technology Press
8581 154th Avenue NE
Redmond, WA 98052
www.redtechpress.com

Library of Congress Catalog Card No: applied for

ISBN 0-9672981-3-X

Printed and bound in the United States of America.

9 8 7 6 5 4 3 2 1

Distributed by
Independent Publishers Group
814 N. Franklin St.
Chicago, IL 60610
www.ipgbook.com

Product and company names mentioned herein may be the trademarks of their respective owners.

In the preparation of this book, both the author and the publisher have made every effort to provide current, correct, and comprehensible information. Nevertheless, inadvertent errors can occur and software and the principles and regulations concerning business often change. Furthermore, the application and impact of principles, rules, and laws can vary widely from case to case because of the unique facts involved. For these reasons, the author and publisher specifically disclaim any liability or loss that is incurred as a consequence of the use and application, directly or indirectly, of any information presented in this book. If legal or other expert assistance is needed, the services of a professional should be sought.

While there are many people the authors would like to thank, Sydney McGrath of Paige Data Management deserves special recognition for taking the time to share her knowledge and opinions at a crucial point in the book's development.

Contents at a Glance

Contents

Step 2   Develop a Content Strategy   17

Step 5   Create Your Web Site   95

Step 8   Deploy Your Web Site   193

Appendix   Set Up Your Web Site on a Local Web Server   217

INTRODUCTION

One problem with many books about Microsoft FrontPage 2000 is this: They're only about FrontPage. At first blush, that seems right. But it's really not. The whole point of FrontPage is to help you easily make a successful Web site, to reach your visitors with effective Web pages conveying the information they want to know.

Doing this requires a certain amount of information about the FrontPage program. But people need more than just descriptions of what commands do and explanations of dialog box buttons. People need information about how to create a Web site. And for this reason, the *Effective Executive's Guide to FrontPage Web Sites* takes a different tack. This book focuses on the process of creating a Web site, breaking down the work into eight distinct steps.

Using this approach, we pick a single construction method for building a Web site and then follow that method through from start to finish. Such an approach means we don't provide encyclopedic coverage of the FrontPage program.

We think breaking the process of creating a Web site into steps works better for the typical FrontPage user—and especially for the business professional who never aspires to become a FrontPage expert or professional Web site creator. Breaking the process into steps forces us (the authors and the reader) to focus on the final product. And breaking the process into steps also lets us create a book that filters everything we *could* say about FrontPage into just what the executive user *should* know.

What This Book Assumes About You

This book makes two assumptions about you. First, the book assumes that you're not and don't want to become a FrontPage expert. Rather, we assume you're a professional working in business, a nonprofit organization, or perhaps public service. We assume that you want to use FrontPage to build and enhance the Web sites you make.

The book also assumes that you're familiar working with the Microsoft Windows operating system. In the pages that follow, as a result, you won't get detailed information about how to choose menu commands or select dialog box buttons and boxes. If you don't already possess this knowledge, you'll need to acquire it either by using the online help available in Windows, by getting a quick tutorial from someone such as a co-worker, or by reading a good introductory book.

How This Book Is Organized

This book breaks the process of building a FrontPage Web site into the following eight steps:

Step 1: Learn the Logic

The best place to start a discussion of building a Web site with FrontPage is with information about how the Internet and Web work, why it makes sense to have a Web site, and what makes Web sites effective. In Step 1, we provide this information.

Step 2: Develop a Content Strategy

Probably the single most important step for you, the executive user, is determining the purpose of the Web site, and what kind of content is required to fulfill this purpose. Step 2 helps you accomplish this task by providing you with some common goals for Web sites, suggestions to help you determine the goals for your Web site, and some methodologies for developing your content.

Step 3: Lay a Foundation

Once you understand how Web sites work and have a content strategy, your next step is to prepare the foundation of your Web site by getting a domain name and locating a company to host your site.

Step 4: Collect and Organize Your Content

After deciding upon the purpose and content for your Web site, it's time to actually gather content together and organize it for use on your site. Besides simply collecting existing content, this also involves creating or digitizing new content, creating a central location to store content, establishing a file naming convention to use on your Web site, organizing your content, and drawing up a plan for your Web site.

Step 5: Create Your Web Site

The actual process of creating a Web site page-by-page begins with this Step 5, and we walk you through all the most important aspects of the process. This includes setting up your Web site in FrontPage, understanding the FrontPage interface, managing files in FrontPage, creating basic Web pages, and coordinating the work of multiple users when creating the site.

Step 6: Polish Your Pages

Once you've created your Web site, you should refine your Web pages to make them more effective and professional. In Step 6, we cover a number of special tasks that you should perform to polish your home page, ways of making the pages in your Web site more consistent and effective, and how to create tables and advanced layouts.

Step 7: Add Interactivity to Your Web Site

You can add interactivity to your Web site by creating user feedback forms, search forms, or discussion groups using FrontPage. Web stores aren't as easily created using FrontPage; however, in Step 7 we discuss the various methods you can use to create a Web store and how to choose a method that's suitable for your company.

Step 8: Deploy Your Web Site

The last step in the Web site creation process is the actual deployment of your site. This includes testing the Web site for errors, publishing it to the Internet, submitting your Web site to search engines, and publicizing your site elsewhere—both on and off the Internet. These tasks are all covered in Step 8, along with monitoring your site for errors after it is posted and tracking the amount and kinds of visitors that your site receives.

NOTE   *In addition to the eight steps, or chapters, described in the preceding paragraphs, the* Effective Executive's Guide to FrontPage Web Sites *also includes an Appendix, "Set Up Your Web Site on a Local Server," which helps you configure a Web server on your local network to store your Web site while you create it, and a Glossary of FrontPage and Web site terms.*

Conventions Used in This Book

This book uses three conventions worth mentioning here. The first is this. We view this book as a conversation among professionals. That means the pronoun *we* refers to us, the authors. And that means the pronoun *you* refers to you, the reader. In this case, this conversation style means you will frequently see the pronoun *we*, because two of us, Gerend and Nelson, wrote the book. Although *we* has sometimes been used as a stilted self-reference by writers, please don't take it that way. Think of us as workshop presenters or discussion group facilitators, with jackets off and ties loosened. Think of us, in other words, as colleagues. Think of this book as a conversation.

Another convention is that we call the main chapters of the book *steps*. The benefit of doing this is that it lets us focus on and emphasize the process of creating a Web site. But, unfortunately, there's a slight problem with this convention. We also want to provide numbered step-by-step instructions in the chapters, or steps, of the book. Whenever some task can't be described in a sentence or two, in fact, we'll use numbered steps to make sure you can follow the discussion. So this "chapters-called-steps" convention may confuse matters. If we say that "in the preceding step, we described how to do such-and-such," are we referring to the preceding chapter? Or a preceding numbered step? You see the difficulty.

Here's what we've come up with. Whenever we use the term *step* to refer to a chapter, we'll just give you the entire step name. For example, if we say that in "Step 2: Develop a Content Strategy" we describe how to do such-and-such, you'll know what we mean. If we don't give you the step name, you'll know we're talking about the preceding numbered step.

A third convention concerns references to the buttons and boxes in FrontPage windows and dialog boxes. Even though they don't appear that way onscreen, this book capitalizes the initial letter of the words that label buttons and boxes. For example, the box that is actually labeled "Save as type" gets referenced in these pages as the Save As Type box. The initial caps, then, will be a signal to you that we're referring to a label.

Step 1

LEARN THE LOGIC

Featuring:

- What Is the Internet?
- How Do Web Pages Work?
- Introducing HTML Code
- Why It Makes Sense to Have a Web Site
- What Makes a Good Web Site?

While the Internet and the Web may seem Byzantine and confusing, the basics are actually pretty simple. Before we launch into the reasons for setting up a Web site, it's important to gain an understanding of the Internet and its many methods of communication. In this step, you'll find out how Web pages work, determine what makes Web sites effective, and learn why it makes sense to have one. When you're finished with this step, you'll have all the background knowledge necessary to start the process of building a Web site for your company or organization.

What Is the Internet?

The Internet is a worldwide amalgamation of computers that are capable of "talking" to each other over some form of network connection. As such, the Internet is very similar to the public phone network; and in fact a large amount of Internet traffic is carried over the same physical cables as our telephone systems.

To use the Internet, you must connect to it. Once connected, there are a number of ways of communicating over it, such as by sending e-mail messages, browsing Web pages, or by using newsgroups, chat, or Internet telephones.

Connecting to the Internet

To access the Internet, you first need to connect to it. There are several ways of doing this. If you are a home or small business user, you probably connect to the Internet using a modem. To connect, you dial your Internet service provider (ISP) with your modem, which is connected to a normal telephone line. A server at the ISP answers the phone, and then connects you to the Internet. This method is available anywhere there are phone lines, and is relatively inexpensive (typically $10 to $20 per month). However, it is somewhat slow. A 56-kilobit modem can reach a maximum download speed of 53 kilobits per second (Kbps)—taking about two and a half to three minutes to download a 1 megabyte (MB) file, which is roughly the amount of text in this book and approximately two-thirds of the space on a 1.44MB floppy disk.

NOTE   *Connection speeds are discussed in terms of kilo**bits** per second (Kbps), while the size of files is discussed in kilo**bytes** (KB) or mega**bytes** (MB). They measure the same thing, except that there are eight bits in a byte, or eight kilobits in a kilobyte, making the numbers different by a factor of eight.*

Digital Subscriber Line (DSL) service is a high-speed form of Internet access that is becoming increasingly popular for both home users and small businesses. DSL also uses a normal telephone line, but requires that the telephone company have special digital equipment installed nearby in order to provide service. Thus, DSL isn't available in all areas.

When available, the service provides constant Internet connectivity (there's no need in most DSL services to dial the ISP—you're always connected) that is much faster than a standard analog modem. DSL speeds range from 192Kbps to around 1.5Mbps, with typical speeds starting at around 300 to 600Kbps (faster speeds are usually available for more money). At 300Kbps, a 1MB file takes about 30 seconds to download. DSL typically costs about $50 per month for the lowest speed service up to around $200 per month for the highest speed service available.

DSL requires a DSL router or a DSL bridge—usually (but incorrectly) referred to as modems. (Technically a modem is a device that modulates and demodulates analog signals, and DSL is all digital.) These devices may be included for free when you sign up for service or may cost several hundred dollars. Many can be plugged directly into the uplink port on your network hub to allow computers to easily share the Internet connection.

Cable modems are another increasingly popular form of high-speed Internet access, but they are generally not available for businesses. When available, they are always-on digital connections that work over cable TV lines. Cable modems provide speeds that vary between 300Kbps and 1.5Mbps. Cable modem service usually costs around $40 per month.

Integrated Services Digital Network (ISDN) is a somewhat older high-speed Internet connection that works over (mostly) normal telephone lines (a special ISDN digital connection needs to be configured by the telephone company). ISDN is popular with small businesses because of its wider service coverage (you can often get ISDN where you can't get DSL) and its ability to provide high-speed access. ISDN speeds typically start at 128Kbps and can be increased in increments of 64Kbps up to a maximum of roughly 1Mbps. ISDN costs roughly $40 per month per 64Kbps of bandwidth (data transfer speed). ISDN, like an analog modem, isn't on all the time, but the connection time is so fast that it appears almost instantaneous.

Medium-size companies that need to share an Internet connection with more than about a couple dozen users will need to use a more sophisticated connection option, such as Frame relay. Frame relay and other so-called "leased lines" generally guarantee a certain amount of bandwidth, provide a lot of it, and charge you amply for it. Frame relay service typically is available with 128Kbps of throughput for around $200 per month, or up to 1.5Mbps of throughput for $600 per month.

NOTE   *Wireless solutions are available, but until recently they have been used exclusively for mobile users owing to their very low speeds (9.6Kbps–28.8Kbps) and high per-minute costs. However, speeds are rising, with mobile wireless achieving 128Kbps and fixed wireless service (with roof-mounted antennas) reaching up to 10Mbps. As competition heats up, wireless costs will fall, as will the costs of other forms of Internet connections.*

Sometimes hearing or reading about different throughput speeds can be challenging to interpret. Table 1-1 summarizes the transmission times to move the photograph shown in Figure 1-1. Note that the photograph—one of medium quality such as you might use as a full-page image in a Web page—is roughly 100 kilobytes in size.

Figure 1-1   A photograph in an image editor such as you might use on a Web page.

CONNECTION	THROUGHPUT	TIME TO TRANSMIT
Modem	56.6Kbps	14 seconds
ISDN	128Kbps	6 seconds
Cable modem	300Kbps	2.5 seconds
DSL	600Kbps	1.2 seconds
Frame relay	1.5Mbps	Half a second

Table 1-1   Examples of transmission times for a simple photograph.

Methods of Communication over the Internet

Computers that have an Internet connection can communicate with other computers on the Internet in a number of ways. The most common ways to communicate are via e-mail and the World Wide Web (WWW, or just the Web for short). Other methods that can be useful as a way of promoting your Web site or company include newsgroups, chat rooms, and Internet telephone applications.

E-Mail

E-mail works like a virtual U.S. Postal Service. You write an e-mail message in an e-mail program—just like you might write a letter using a word processor or a pad of paper and a pen. Figure 1-2 shows an example of the Microsoft Outlook Express e-mail message window.

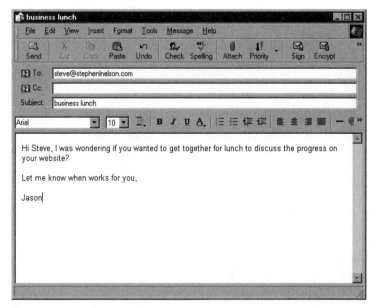

Figure 1-2 An e-mail message.

To send the message, you connect to the Internet and click the Send/Receive button in your mail software to deliver the message to your e-mail "post office" (mail server). This is analogous to getting in your car and driving to the post office to drop off a letter. At both the virtual and real post offices, the next step is to sort the message and deliver it to the post office nearest to the recipient. The recipient then has to connect to the Internet and download his or her new message—like driving to a post office to pick up mail at a post office box.

The Web

The Web works quite a bit differently from e-mail. A Web site consists of a number of specially formatted documents called Web pages that are linked to each other by hyperlinks and that are sitting on a server connected to the Internet. To view a Web site, you use your Web browser program to request a specific Web page from the server storing the Web site. You do this by either clicking a hyperlink or entering the address (known as a uniform resource locator, or URL) of the specific Web site. The Web server responds by sending the requested page across the Internet to your Web browser, which then reads the document, formats it appropriately, and displays it onscreen. Figure 1-3 shows an example Web page.

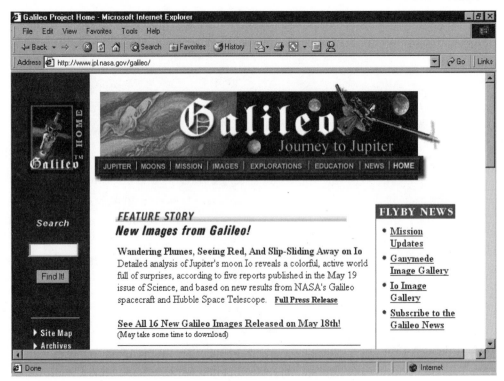

Figure 1-3 A Web page.

The Web has quickly become the most popular part of the Internet for three reasons. The first is the flexibility of the medium. Just about anything can be done in a Web page with a little ingenuity—from online shopping to online gaming. The second is how easy it is to use. Web browsers are fairly self-explanatory, and navigation consists of pointing at links and clicking a mouse. The third reason is that companies and advertising are welcome on the Web—something that can't really be said of other parts of the Internet. When companies try to advertise on other parts of the Internet, it is usually met with displeasure (although as described in "Step 8: Deploy Your Web Site," other parts of the Internet can be used to draw visitors to your Web site, if done appropriately).

Newsgroups and Chat Groups

Newsgroups are very much like virtual bulletin boards. Anyone can post a message on the newsgroup for anyone else to see. All messages are stored on the news server, and you download only those messages you want to read. Figure 1-4 shows an example of a message in a newsgroup. Newsgroups are organized on different topics and subjects of interest, providing a fairly dynamic medium for communication.

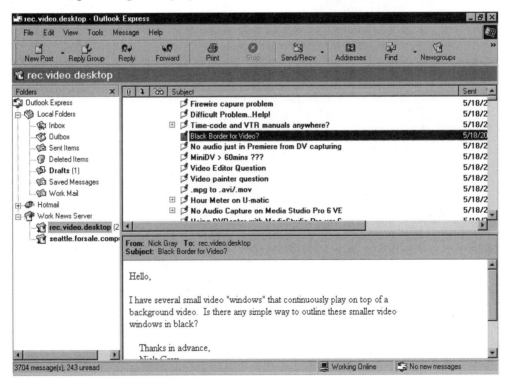

Figure 1-4 A message in a newsgroup.

Chat provides a way to have a real-time, text-based conversation with other users across the Internet. You chat with other people in a so-called chat room, which is basically a chat server that facilitates computer connections. You communicate by typing your message, which then appears instantly on your chat partner's screen.

Instant Messaging

A similar type of real-time, text-based Internet communication method is instant messaging—as provided by applications such as AOL Instant Messenger, ICQ, and MSN Messenger. These programs act as a sort of Internet-based text telephone. When you go online, you can determine which of your friends are online, and then contact them via the software and conduct a one-to-one text-based chat. This is similar to normal chat software, except that conversations are usually private and you can easily find your friends or colleagues when they're online. Figure 1-5 shows an example of a conversation using an instant messaging program.

Figure 1-5   A real-time conversation using MSN Messenger.

Internet Telephone Services

Internet telephone software packages take the chat concept a step further. These software programs, such as CU-SeeMe, Net2Phone, or Microsoft NetMeeting, provide real-time voice (and occasionally video) communication with other users who are connected to the Internet and running the same software. Some programs even provide the ability to call normal telephones through the Internet. The chief reasons to use Internet telephone programs are to take advantage of enhanced communication features, such as video teleconferencing (videophone); have the ability to view another user's computer screen while talking; or save on long-distance telephone costs.

How Do Web Pages Work?

A Web page is simply a text document with special codes in it that tell a Web browser how to format and display the contents of the page. In addition to the special formatting, Web pages can also contain embedded images (that show up in the page onscreen but are stored separately on the server) and links (hyperlinks) to other pages.

In the old days, all Web pages were created manually in hypertext markup language (HTML), which is discussed briefly in the next section. Although some people still create Web pages this way, it is far easier and faster to use a program such as FrontPage 2000 to create Web pages graphically—without having to write any code.

Introducing HTML Code

It's highly probable that you'll never want to write a Web page from scratch in HTML, but it is useful to know what HTML looks like. Although FrontPage 2000 allows you to easily work without touching a line of code, it helps to see how your pages are actually built and know that you could possibly add code yourself if need be. You'll also have a better idea about what someone you hire to perform HTML editing and coding is actually doing.

To begin, let's look at a simple sentence in HTML code. For example, every programmer's first assignment is to create code that displays the phrase "hello world," so let's do that in HTML.

```
<html>
<p>hello world</p>
</html>
```

This is a complete Web page. It's made up of two tags, which are the basic building blocks of an HMTL document. The first tag, <html>, states that the document is an HTML document and marks the beginning of the Web page. The second half of this tag, </html>, comes at the end of the document and signifies the end of the page. The second tag, <p>, signifies a new paragraph. The actual paragraph in this case is simply "hello world," and the paragraph ends with the second half of the paragraph tag, </p>.

TIP   *All HTML tags begin with a left angle bracket (<) and end with a right angle bracket (>). They usually begin and end similarly to the <html> and <p> tags— the end of the tag is the same as the beginning, except for the addition of a slash (/). For example, </p> closes the <p> tag, ending it.*

Now let's try to decipher something a little more complex. The next page includes an image and a hyperlink. Figure 1-6 shows what this page looks like in a Web browser. Here's the code for it:

```
<html>

<p><img src="images/un.gif"></p>
<p>hello <a> href="http://www.un.org">world</a></p>

</html>
```

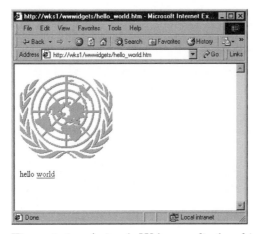

Figure 1-6   A simple Web page displayed in a Web browser.

Notice that the code includes an additional paragraph, which contains the <img> tag. This is the inline image tag (which means it is an image displayed in a Web page instead of an image that you can download), and it works like this: The tag starts with <img to indicate that it's an inline image, and then it contains one or more attributes. The only attribute used here is the src attribute, which contains the URL (address) of the image to be displayed. In this case, the image is the images/un.gif image. The tag ends with a right angle bracket (>).

NOTE   *The acronym URL stands for uniform resource locator. Essentially, URLs identify files by name and give their precise location.*

Notice also that in the middle of the "hello world" paragraph there is now a hyperlink. The hyperlink tag starts with <a> and ends with </a>, and in between are the attributes of the hyperlink and the text to which the hyperlink is attached. In this case, the only attribute is the href attribute (which is the URL of the hyperlink). You can use the href attribute by typing href= and then entering the URL to use, enclosed in quotes.

The tag is partially closed by the right angle bracket (>) following the href attribute, but don't let this fool you. This is so that the text to which the hyperlink is actually attached, world, isn't thought of as another attribute. The hyperlink tag actually ends after this text with the </a> tag.

NOTE   *There is no* http://www.mycompany.com/ *included in the <img> tag to iden-*
        tify the actual physical location of the image, but this is an important omission.
        Because the URL is missing the first part (http://www.mycompany.com/), *Web*
        browsers assume that it should start in the same directory as the current Web
        page. This is highly desirable because it allows you to move the entire Web site
        to a different location (say, from a local folder to your Internet Web site) and
        still have these links work.

One final comment concerning HTML: If you create this same simple page using FrontPage, you will see some additional HTML codes, or tags. FrontPage sets up a more complex page, including header information that isn't displayed (using the <head> tag) and the title of the Web page (using the <title> tag). FrontPage also delineates the body of the page (using the <body> tag) and provides some additional information about the page's contents using meta tags (<meta>). Meta tags provide information to search engines and use the <meta name="keywords"> tag so that search engines can more easily and accurately index the contents of a Web site.

New Web Page Technologies

In addition to HTML pages, a number of new technologies have been developed for Web pages. Even if these technologies don't apply to your Web site initially, it's good to know that if you need something more sophisticated than that provided by FrontPage 2000, the capability exists. The following list describes relevant Web page technologies and what they do.

• Dynamic HTML: Introduces movement and the ability to react to a user's actions to Web pages. For example, text may highlight when a user moves the mouse over it. Mainly useful for adding visual flair to a Web site, DHTML can be created directly within FrontPage 2000, which makes it fairly easy to use.

- Macromedia Flash and Shockwave: These two products allow professional Web developers to create fancy effects and interactivity on a Web page—like DHTML, except more powerful and flexible. Web browsers don't natively support Flash or Shockwave, so a browser plug-in must be downloaded before users can view the effects (although many users will already have the plug-in installed from viewing other Web sites). If you need more interactivity and control than is possible with standard Web pages or pages with DHTML code in them, consider hiring someone to create a Flash or Shockwave component for your Web site.

- Javascript, Java, and ActiveX: These technologies provide a way of performing complex tasks within a Web page, and can even function as full-featured programs. These technologies are complicated—and using them is best left to a professional Web developer.

- CGI Scripts: This is a technology used on some Web servers to provide server-based features such as visitor counters and discussion groups. FrontPage 2000 in most ways provides all the functionality of CGI Scripts when used on a Web server supporting FrontPage Server Extensions. This saves the cost of hiring a professional Web developer to create scripts for your Web site.

- XML: Stands for Extended Markup Language. XML provides a way of giving detailed content information about a Web page, allowing for more meaningful searching and information gathering.

Why It Makes Sense to Have a Web Site

Although a great deal of exuberance surrounds the Internet and especially the Web, it's fairly easy to identify and describe the handful of reasons why it makes good business sense for your organization to have a Web site.

Advertising

The Web, as you'll see in the pages that follow, let's you create powerful advertisements and publicity for a very modest cost. The quickest way to visualize this is to think of your Web site and its Web pages as substitutes for enhanced versions of any telephone directory advertising that you do now.

It's not an exaggeration to say that anything you can do in a directory listing or advertisement, you can do better and more cheaply using a Web page. You can also more frequently change and update your information.

TIP   *The Web really levels the playing field for small businesses. A small business can create a Web site as good or better in many ways than a larger company's Web site without a large amount of expense or time, giving small businesses an unprecedented ability to compete.*

Publishing

Many organizations are de facto publishers. For example, if your firm or organization creates and distributes brochures, newsletters, product or service literature, or similar items, you actually are publishing. The Web provides a convenient way to complement or even replace this paper-based publishing.

Developing material for publication on the Web doesn't cost any more than developing equivalent material for paper publishing. But with the Web, you don't have the costs of printing or mailing. Furthermore, with the Web, you can update your information quicker.

Information Collection

In addition to the advertising and publishing advantages that the Web offers to organizations, the Web also offers the ability to collect information from the people for whom you advertise and publish. You can put forms right on a Web page to collect information from the visitors to your Web site. You might gather names for a mailing list, get feedback from customers, or take in sales orders.

NOTE   *"Step 7: Add Interactivity to Your Web Site," describes how to use forms to collect information from the people who visit your Web site.*

Transaction Processing

Another advantage of the Web that's of great value is the opportunity for transaction processing. As an extension of the Web's information collection ability, transaction processing lets you use the Web as a virtual store, salesperson, or distribution facility.

Using the Web for transaction processing is considerably trickier than using it for advertising or publishing. Obviously, your Web pages need to list and describe the products you sell. But practically speaking, you need to do more than simply list products or services. Good Web stores have the following features:

- Information about product availability and about the lead times for ordering items that aren't immediately available.

- A variety of ways to track down your products and services so that they are easy to find and buy.

- A shopping cart feature that lets customers build a list of the items they want.

- A checkout feature that lets customers easily order all the items in their shopping cart. (It's during this checkout process, of course, that customers provide their credit card numbers and shipping instructions.)

- A non-Web way for resolving problems the Web store can't handle, such as lost or damaged goods.

This book doesn't spend much time on setting up a transaction processing Web site. This process is really beyond the skill set of most business professionals—principally because you need to be able to search and then show your product inventory database on your Web pages. Nevertheless, "Step 7: Add Interactivity to Your Web Site," does describe in specific terms about how you can set up simple transaction-processing capabilities and then in more general terms about how you can use a third-party Web store hosting service if transaction processing is what you need or want.

NOTE   *Regardless of what you think about* www.amazon.com, *you should visit their Web site—even if you compete with them (perhaps especially if you compete with them). They've done an impressive job of providing numerous paths to find their products and different ways to search through their inventory. For example, they have several different bestseller lists for Microsoft Excel books, each listing books in a different order for a different group of Excel readers. We strongly suspect their several bestseller lists of Excel books, each really an alternative path to the same products, boost their sales of Excel books because they make it more likely someone will find them.*

What Makes a Good Web Site?

No matter what you choose to use your Web site for—advertising, publishing, information collection, or transaction processing—three main features differentiate effective sites: useful content, easy navigation, and aesthetic appeal. The following sections briefly identify how to spot an effective Web site, and by extension, how to create one.

Useful Content

More than anything else, useful content is the single most important feature of an effective Web site. It doesn't matter how well designed a Web site is, if it doesn't have useful content, the Web site is worthless.

Besides having worthwhile content, good Web sites also bring visitors back repeatedly. Generally, visitors return to Web sites to view new or changed information or to view information that remains useful, perhaps as a reference source. Having both consistently useful content *and* frequently changing or new information is ideal, but both approaches are also effective by themselves.

Dynamic Content

Web sites that make use of dynamic content to keep visitors coming back require more work than Web sites that remain largely unchanged, but also tend to result in people coming to the site more frequently.

There are lots of ways that effective Web sites make use of dynamic content to entice visitors back to their Web sites. A company or organization may choose to post updated schedules and event listings or information on special sales. Other potential sources for updated content include press releases, reports, or news about the company or organization.

Content doesn't have to be limited to strictly company information either. A Web site that provides freshly updated news, a regular column, tips, or advice on a subject of interest to its visitors will get return visitors. Even if people weren't explicitly coming to the Web site to buy something or to get information about the company or organization, once they're at your site, many will investigate further.

Another approach that may work for some Web sites is to dole out new information about something to build suspense and interest—and keep visitors coming back. Usually this approach is taken when releasing a major new product or event. However, wise webmasters use this trick sparingly so as not to annoy visitors.

Static Content

Consistently useful information is always good to have in a Web site. A Web site for a nonprofit organization might have a reference library of useful documents it has prepared, or simply directions to its place of business. Companies selling products may post their product catalogs, manuals, or support information. Static content isn't something to be ashamed of—the goal of a Web site is to provide visitors with the information they seek, and if that information doesn't change, that's fine.

Easy Navigation

Although good content is the most important feature of a good Web site, it can be seriously hampered by poor site layout. Not only should visitors be able to easily find what they're looking for but the organization of Web pages and hyperlinks should also give visitors a good idea of the site's contents at a glance from the home page. Creating an effective organization for your Web site is covered extensively in "Step 4: Collect and Organize Your Content," and implementing it on your home page is discussed specifically in "Step 5: Create Your Web Site."

Visual Appeal

Aesthetics is very important for Web sites, but it is also the part of Web site creation that is most overemphasized by many companies. Professional artists and programmers are hired to create custom interfaces using trendy technologies, such as Macromedia's Flash, and altogether too much time, money, and resources are spent making Web sites look sophisticated instead of filling them with good content.

A flashy Web site may grab the attention of visitors, but a clean and simple site can be just as effective (or more so), and much less expensive to create and maintain. Complex effects and graphics can also make a site slow to download and confusing to use. Not to mention that sophisticated Web page programming can be incompatible with older browsers, along with some handheld devices and stand-alone Internet appliances.

Summary

This step introduced the Internet, Web sites, and how Web pages work. Now that you know about the most popular methods of communication on the Internet—e-mail, the Web, and newsgroups—have seen some HTML code, and have learned about the three most important features in effective Web sites—content, layout, and visual appeal—it's time to start developing your Web site.

In "Step 2: Develop a Content Strategy," you'll learn some of the most common reasons why companies create Web sites, how to determine the goal for your company or organization's Web site, and some methodologies for developing content for your Web site.

Step 2

DEVELOP A CONTENT STRATEGY

Featuring:

- Common Web Site Goals

- Determining Your Web Site's Goals

- Methodologies for Developing Your Content

Once you understand the Internet and the Web in a general way—you're ready to decide what you want to do with your own Web site. You can easily start by looking at what's out there, as discussed in the pages that follow. You can also ask and answer some simple questions that allow you to develop a content strategy for your Web site. Finally, we think you can use an iterative development methodology that lets you get started now and get smarter about your content later on, as discussed at the end of this step.

NOTE *We're using the phrase "content strategy" to describe what information you want to share and maintain using your Web site.*

Common Web Site Goals

A good place to start your own work on a content strategy is by looking at what other organizations—both organizations like your own and those completely different from yours—have done with their Web sites. Even though the popularity of the Internet and the World Web Wide are relatively recent, there are many examples available of what you should and shouldn't do with your own Web site. The following sections present some common goals for Web sites to give you a better idea about how to form your own content strategy.

Advertising Your Company or Organization

Advertising a company or organization represents one of the most common reasons for creating a Web site. Such advertising informs outsiders about your organization's purpose, activities, and future. This kind of institutional advertising falls into at least five categories: general information, current activities information, location and direction information, financial information, and contact information.

General Information

General information describes what your firm or organization does, what distinguishes it from other similar organizations, and in short, what makes the organization noteworthy. Nonprofit organizations, for example, may want to discuss the organization's purpose and mission. Businesses may want to discuss not only their services and products but also their history and any special credentials.

Oftentimes, you'll already have this content in the form of a brochure or print publication that can be adapted for a Web site. (We'll talk about this recycling of content in more detail in "Step 4: Collect and Organize Your Content.") But the general rule is that someone visiting your organization's Web site should come away with the impression that your organization is unique.

NOTE   *A useful idea to consider as you provide this general information is the bookmark rule. Web browsers like Microsoft Internet Explorer and Netscape Navigator let a Web visitor add a Web page address to a list of remembered pages. Internet Explorer calls these pages "favorites," and Netscape Navigator calls these pages "bookmarks." The reason we bring this up here is to suggest this: anything you can do to increase the chances that someone will add your Web site to their list of bookmarks or favorites is worth considering.*

Current Activities Information

If your organization regularly sponsors events, your visitors should usually be able to learn about these events by looking at a calendar or schedule on your Web site.

Consider, too, the possibility of including an archive or history of past activities. In some situations, information about successful past events works well for promoting upcoming events or activities. This archival information might include transcripts of meetings or seminars, pictures from past events, reports on completed projects, and quotations from event participants.

Location and Direction Information

If clients or customers will need to visit your physical location besides visiting your Web site, you may want to include maps and directions on your Web site—especially if they already exist in the form of printed material that can be adapted for use on your Web site. This is particularly true for nonprofit institutions such as churches, synagogues, and mosques; for retailing businesses such as restaurants and stores; and professional service firms such as medical clinics and law offices. In all of these cases, your organization may regularly be providing location and direction information over the phone or via mail.

NOTE *Many smaller organizations may be able to identify useful content merely by querying the receptionist. The questions that callers ask most often should probably be answered on your Web site. For example, if people call asking for directions, location information really does belong on your Web site.*

Financial Information

Many organizations are required by law to provide financial information to the public. Still others, either by tradition or to foster a policy of openness and transparency, provide financial information voluntarily. If your organization wants to provide this information, a Web site is another way to distribute this data, as shown in Figure 2-1.

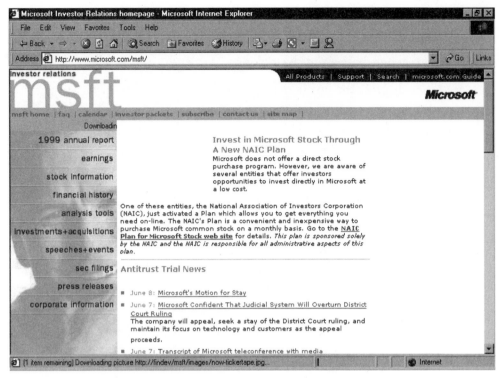

Figure 2-1   The Investor Relations page at Microsoft's Web site.

Contact Information

Your Web site should provide appropriate content information so that if visitors have questions or want to contact someone for more information, they'll be able to. Typically, firms provide an e-mail address in addition to mailing and street address information and telephone and fax numbers.

NOTE   *While a Web site is one of the best ways to advertise, usually you need to put a little effort into advertising the Web site before it can be truly effective. While this may sound paradoxical—advertising an advertisement, it's important to recognize that Web sites often act as a sort of second stage of advertisement. Once people realize that they want more information (either because they're explicitly looking for something or because you've attracted their attention through some other form of advertising), they can go to your Web site and find all the information they want. That's powerful. But before your site can be effective, you need visitors. "Step 8: Deploy Your Web Site" describes tactics to employ for performing this first-stage advertising for your Web site.*

Selling or Advertising a Product or Service

A Web site designed to advertise or sell a product or service differs somewhat in its content and focus as compared to a Web site designed to primarily advertise the firm or organization itself. Product advertising Web sites focus on presenting product information, pictures, and ordering information, while Web sites focusing on advertising a firm or organization tend to emphasize the purpose, activities, and future of the company over its products or services. However, there is a fair amount of overlap between the two, and most Web sites advertising a product or service will also have some emphasis on the company itself, albeit to a lesser degree. The following sections identify content typically used for advertising a product or service.

Product or Service Information

An online catalog of products or services arguably is the meat of any Web site attempting to advertise a product or service. You'll probably find that it's most effective to summarize each product so that visitors can quickly get a feel for the product or service and what's good about it, similar to the way a print catalog is usually created.

With the practically unlimited space available on a Web site, however, it's often desirable to have detailed information available for those visitors who are looking for more specifics. Ideally, all the information available on a given product or service should be accessible from your Web site, including third-party reviews, technical documents, and support information.

Asus's Web site *(http://www.asus.com.tw)* is a good example of a Web site that includes just about every bit of information a customer would want about a product, as shown in Figure 2-2. Although they could be a bit better about summarizing and reducing visual clutter, it's nonetheless an effective product advertisement site.

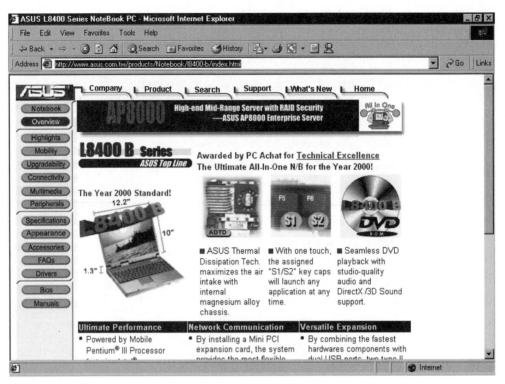

Figure 2-2   The product information page for an Asus laptop.

Pictures of Products or Services

While pictures may not always be worth a thousand words, they can be extremely useful when trying to advertise a product or service. Usually one or two good pictures per product is adequate, though certain products or services may lend themselves to having a small photo gallery available (in a separate page) for curious visitors.

Ordering Information

Your Web site may not be a full e-commerce site—a site that allows for online orders—but it's still a good idea to present potential customers with easy ways to buy your products or services. This can include the locations where your products or services are available, price lists, a phone number for placing orders, a form that visitors can use to place an order that will be processed via e-mail, or full online ordering ability with a shopping cart and credit card processing.

NOTE *Setting up an e-commerce site can be very involved. See "Step 7: Add Interactivity to Your Web Site" for more information.*

Support Links or Information

Depending on your product or service, it may be highly desirable to feature links to online product support information or customer support. Many potential customers check specifically on the quality of support for a given product before making a purchase, and thus having a helpful product support section on your site could help convince visitors to become patrons.

Disseminating Information

Perhaps the greatest strength of the Web is how well it's suited to passing on information. No printing costs are involved; information can be changed as frequently as necessary; pictures, audio, and even video can be included with text; and there are no real limits on how much information can be posted on a Web site. The Web truly is an almost ideal publishing medium.

There are many different reasons that your organization may find it valuable to create a Web site designed to share information with your visitors.

One reason is the need to streamline the day-to-day operations of a company. The Web site of the U.S. Internal Revenue Service (IRS) is an excellent example of streamlining (see Figure 2-3). By making just about every bit of tax information available online, the IRS reduces the burden on its phone staff, reduces the number of taxpayer errors on the tax returns it reviews, and also presumably builds goodwill toward the organization. UPS and Federal Express are two other examples of companies that streamline their businesses by providing valuable information to their visitors (they post sending and tracking information).

Figure 2-3   The Small Business Corner page of the IRS Web site.

A nonprofit organization may use its Web site to educate the public about issues in which the organization is involved, helping the organization make progress on the issues while at the same time increasing public awareness of the issues and the organization.

Firms and organizations can also disseminate information as a way to entice visitors to their Web sites, acting in a way as a great form of advertising. When valuable information is shared (and appropriately advertised, as described in "Step 8: Deploy Your Web Site"), people will be drawn to your site, which increases the exposure of your site. If you then strategically place links to your product or company information, you can generate increased traffic to the parts of your site that directly benefit your organization. This is a very powerful advertising technique because it actually offers something of value to visitors while at the same time exposing them to your Web site.

Chances are good that if your company or organization is creating a Web site primarily aimed at disseminating information, you probably already know exactly what content you'll use. However, if you're using an online newsletter or information source as a way to draw visitors to your Web site, you might be able to use some help. If this is the case, here are some suggestions:

- Create a Web site that people will find a valuable source of information by drawing upon your company or organization's unique knowledge or perspective. This offers visitors something of value that they can't get elsewhere.

- If your company manufactures or sells a product, create some tutorials or product tips on your Web site to help customers make better use of the product.

- Create a newsletter related to your business's occupation. This newsletter can contain industry news, opinion articles, case studies, and product reviews (of your company's products most likely).

- Provide information on activities or tasks that are slightly outside the scope of your company's products. This can help to make your company's Web site a central hub, which visitors can use to find related information of interest to them.

TIP   *One way to determine the kind of content that would attract visitors to your Web site is to conduct a survey—most likely on your Web site, but possibly via a print or other offline medium. See "Step 7: Add Interactivity to Your Web Site" for more information on creating survey forms.*

Generating Online Advertising Revenue

Many firms and organizations can help support the cost of a Web site (or even make it a profit source) by allowing other companies to advertise on their Web site, or by earning commissions from referring visitors to online Web stores. Just as magazines are largely advertiser supported, it's quite possible to run a profitable online magazine or newsletter supported largely or exclusively by banner ads and affiliation programs on your site.

Yahoo! *(www.yahoo.com)* is an example of such a Web site (see Figure 2-4). Even though the ads placed on the site aren't as obtrusive as some, because of the volume of visitors to the site, Yahoo! makes money from those visitors who click on the ads. Advertisers typically pay a small amount for each user who clicks on an ad. And a large number of visitors means a reasonable amount of income.

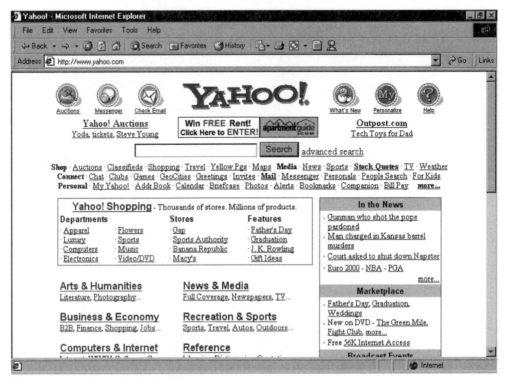

Figure 2-4   Yahoo!'s Web site.

The key to making money from advertisements on your Web site is getting enough visitors to your Web site to generate a large number of click-throughs (instances where a visitor clicks on an ad). To do this, you'll probably need some enticing content—possibly an online newsletter, tutorials, or free downloads relating to your products or industry. Because of this need for a large number of visitors, you might want to hold off on placing ads on your Web site until your site is established and generating a significant amount of traffic, and then choose the ads that are most appropriate to your visitors.

Selling Digital Content

If your company or organization provides unusually valuable content, you may be able to charge Web site visitors to access or use the information. This approach requires additional development effort, however, as discussed in "Step 7: Add Interactivity to Your Web Site."

NOTE   *Nobody likes to pay for information. If you can make your Web site work without charging for access, do so—your site will have more visitors, fewer irritated visitors, and eliminate the added expense and hassle involved with setting up and maintaining a restricted access Web site. However, if your information really is valuable, charging for its access may be the only way to go. (If it's too valuable, you may not want to entrust it to a Web site, since it's not difficult for disgruntled or unethical subscribers to share their username and password with others.)*

Although most content isn't very amenable to selling over the Internet, some types of content can be sold online. For example, data that your company or organization has collected that is unique and valuable can be very saleable. A fairly sky-high example of this is *www.spaceimaging.com* (shown in Figure 2-5), which sells spy satellite photos.

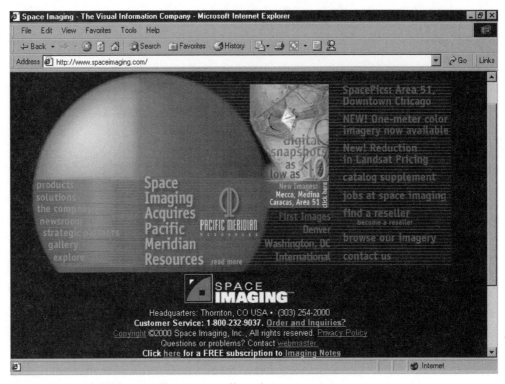

Figure 2-5   A Web site selling spy satellite photos.

High-quality information that your company or organization used to charge for can also often be sold via a Web site. An example of this would be *www.worldbookonline.com* (shown in Figure 2-6), which sells access to its World Book Encyclopedia.

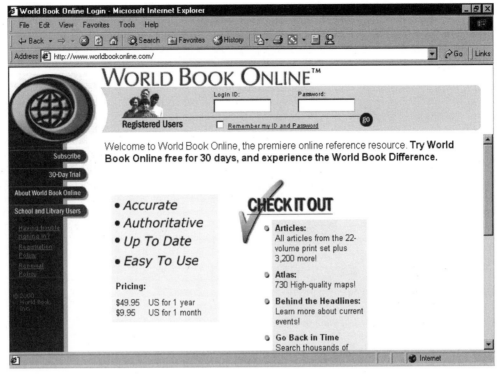

Figure 2-6   The World Book Online Web site.

Professionally created content of interest to visitors, such as high-resolution photos, artwork, sounds, or music, can often be sold online. Instead of treating your content as products to sell, you can instead treat it as a service to which visitors can subscribe. An example of this kind of site is *www.arttoday.com*, shown in Figure 2-7, which sells access to its images and clip art.

Figure 2-7   The ArtToday Web site.

Supporting a Product

Customer and technical support are two business activities that can significantly eat into profits. It's expensive to maintain a staff to handle customer and technical support (or divert resources from employees with other job functions), pay the expense of a toll-free number, and deal with unsatisfied and disappointed customers.

Creating a Web site or portion of a Web site dedicated to customer or technical support won't eliminate the need for customer and technical support. However, it can help reduce the need for traditional offline (usually phone-based) support by empowering customers to solve the most common problems themselves, or at least streamline the support process. As with everything relating to Web site construction, each company will have unique content requirements, but here are some suggestions.

A List of Frequently Asked Questions (FAQ)

Creating a list of answers to the most commonly asked questions may lower the number of customer support calls you receive, or at least make some customers happier because the availability of instant help eliminated a phone call—and a wait on hold.

A Knowledge Base of Support Articles

Another way to reduce your support costs is to create a knowledge base of articles addressing potential problems your customers might encounter. One way to build up a knowledge base is to encourage your support staff to write up an article for every problem they encounter, unless a knowledge base article already addresses the problem. (This is what Microsoft Corporation does.) All articles can then be placed on the Web site along with a search form that allows users to search the knowledge base for a specific article, as shown in Figure 2-8.

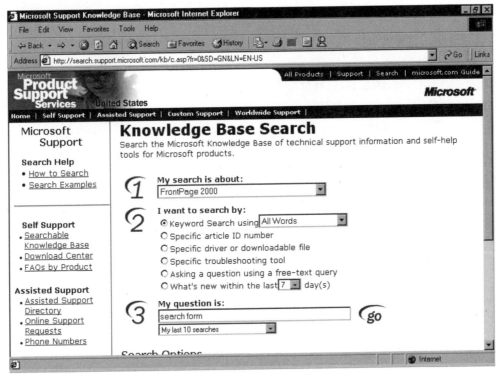

Figure 2-8   The Knowledge Base Search section of Microsoft's Product Support Services Web site.

Contact Information

A product support Web site won't eliminate the need for traditional means of support, so you need to consider providing customers with the contact information for your customer and technical support staff. Although this usually means a telephone number, you may want to encourage visitors to preferentially e-mail the support staff, as this eliminates any wait time users might have with phone support, reduces phone bills, and allows your company's support staff to more efficiently respond to requests.

Online Discussion Groups

FrontPage 2000 provides the ability to create discussion groups on a Web site, allowing visitors and company personnel to post and reply to messages, much like a Web-based newsgroup. (See "Step 1: Learn the Logic," for more information on newsgroups.)

The advantage of discussion groups is that users can often get help from other users of the discussion group, reducing the load on your company's support staff and also expediting the resolution of the user's problem. More than just resolving problems, discussion groups are also an excellent way for users to share experiences, tips, and other information related to your product, service, or company.

Because discussions aren't conducted in real-time, however, they can't replace more immediate forms of support, such as e-mail, chat, or telephone support. Figure 2-9 shows an excellent discussion group Web site dedicated to Ulead's MediaStudio Pro (although Ulead did not create the site), one that has provided users with lots of information for which they would otherwise have turned to technical support.

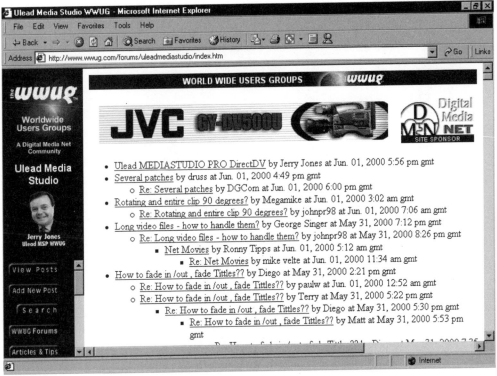

Figure 2-9   A discussion group Web site dedicated to Ulead's MediaStudio Pro.

Chat-Based Online Support

This is a relatively new form of providing customer support, and it's not for every company. A chat-based support system allows users to contact support personnel in a real-time, text-based chat session across the Internet. The advantages of this method are that it's generally cheaper than phone-based support (no telephone costs or need for additional phone lines), more efficient (personnel can often handle multiple users at once), and more convenient for some users (many users prefer to wait online instead of on hold).

While chat-based online support amounts to a fairly effective way of supporting customers, it's not natively supported in FrontPage 2000, so you need to turn to third-party solutions if your company desires this functionality. Figure 2-10 shows an example (HumanClick at *http://www.humanclick.com*) and "Step 7: Add Interactivity to Your Web Site" discusses chat solutions also.

Figure 2-10 An online support chat window as provided by HumanClick's software.

Product Manuals

Placing online versions of product manuals on the Web site makes it easier for users to find information without contacting customer support, especially if they've lost or don't have the manual handy.

Product Updates

Depending on what kind of products your company deals with, you may want to place product updates on your Web site for users to download, or give information on how users can get updated versions of your products.

Complementing a Curriculum

Any parent of a school-aged child knows that most schools make a lot of printouts, and children inevitably lose some of them. Students of professional schools are also familiar with the inconvenience of lost papers.

The Web can help out parents, teachers, and students by serving as a sort of online publication location where just about anything that normally would appear in print can be found (see Figure 2-11). This reduces the amount of paper wasted by handouts, helps students to get assignments done, makes it easier for parents to get their children to finish assignments, and generally helps students and parents to access the information they need.

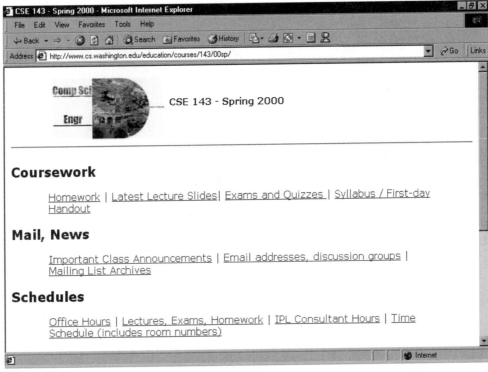

Figure 2-11 An example of a simple Web page designed to accompany a class.

Ideally, a Web site designed to complement a curriculum or school should contain anything that would ordinarily be printed, but here are some specific suggestions and ideas:

- Make current assignments available for convenient access.

- Post the due dates for assignments, test dates, special lectures, and anything else of importance.

- If the class involves lectures, consider making copies of the lectures available online. Making lecture slides available can also serve to increase the perceived value of the class.

- Include information on how grades are calculated and other background information, such as attendance policy and office hours.

- Post current course descriptions and class times and dates for easy reference.

- List registration information and instructions on the Web site. Not all schools will want to make online registration available because of the complexity and cost involved (it generally requires hiring an outside contractor to set up online registration systems), but most will want to post information on the proper way to register.

- Post cafeteria menus and prices.

- List the faculty, their credentials, and contact information.

- Post specific information about the school, its history, and its future. (See the "Advertising Your Company or Organization" section earlier in this step for more ideas on what kind of content to present.)

Determining Your Web Site's Goals

After reviewing, considering, and perhaps exploring the content strategies that other Web publishers have chosen, it's time to determine the goals for your own Web site. Practically speaking, of course, you may choose to mimic some other Web publisher—at least initially. Even when that's the case, however, you may find it helpful to answer the following four questions:

1. **What should the site accomplish?**

   Businesses and organizations don't just make Web sites because it seems like a good way to appear technologically savvy (well, *most* companies don't). They make Web sites to accomplish something—for example, advertising the company, selling a product or service, acting as an online newsletter, providing customer support, or complementing a teaching curriculum. Although more than one purpose for a Web site is generally the norm, clearly defining what the Web site should accomplish is a vital step in creating an effective Web site.

2. **How is this going to benefit my company or organization?**

   Few companies or organizations can afford to be truly altruistic, so the potential benefits of your Web site need to be kept in mind. A popular and well-designed Web site isn't much good if your company or organization doesn't benefit from it in some way. Keep in mind that there are many ways a company can benefit from a Web site, including increased sales, decreased customer support costs, improved public image, or a better understanding of the company or organization (especially beneficial to nonprofit organizations).

Many companies will find it helpful to write down their answers to the questions presented here so that everyone involved in the project can refer back to them as they create the Web site. This document becomes especially important in "Step 4: Collect and Organize Your Content" when we suggest that you use it as an aid to plan your Web site.

3. **What content should the site contain in order to accomplish the Web site's purpose?**

Once you've determined what you want your Web site to accomplish, it's important to identify what kind of content will help your Web site live up to your company or organization's expectations. If the Web site exists to inform the public about a specific issue that your organization deals with, it's important to have lots of information regarding that issue and not as important to have pictures of all the employees. Your content needs to attract users to your site, keep them there, and entice them to return again. Keep asking whether any potential content will help further the purpose of the Web site—if it doesn't, think twice before spending time and resources on it.

4. **Is the content appropriate for the target audience?**

While it's generally a bad idea to create a Web site that excludes people outside your usual clientele, it is desirable to tailor Web sites to match the typical visitor of the site. For example, a Web site devoted to industry professionals probably doesn't need to talk in basic terms. It can give visitors just the information they need—not information they already know (include a primer for newcomers).

TIP *Do some research on your target audience. Identify the types of people who are most likely to view your site, but make sure not to exclude people too quickly. Some companies find it useful to create personas that embody the different demographics your site is trying to appeal to—several hypothetical users that you can concentrate on when designing your site. Will Betty like the site? Will John find the information he's looking for?*

Methodologies for Developing Your Content

As we wrap up this short discussion of the Web content strategies people usually consider, we'd like to leave you with one last thought. We recommend you more or less take a bulletin board approach to developing your Web content. By this, we mean that you should develop the content for your Web site in much the way that the content for the bulletin board in your coffee room or at your local market is developed.

Following a bulletin board methodology, as you find or create some appropriate Web content, you simply pin the content to the bulletin board—or post the content to your Web site. When content needs to change, you update the content or replace it. If content needs to be removed, you remove it, or unpin it, from the bulletin board.

This bulletin board methodology is somewhat opposite of the strategy taken by larger companies, which is to treat a Web site almost like a software product—something that needs extensive research, development, and testing before it can be rolled out. The advantage of this large-system-development approach is that the Web site usually hits the pavement running strong, which is important for the IPO-focused high-tech companies of today's business world that can get tens of thousands of visitors their first day online.

However, the software product methodology doesn't work as well for smaller businesses and organizations because it delays and may even kill the project if the resources expended in developing the Web site so burden the project that it never gets completed.

Accordingly, we suggest you think about a Web site as something that's constantly under construction, where you post content as it's created or updated, and where you revise as needed, thereby letting your Web site grow and become more polished naturally, almost organically. Since smaller companies probably won't be immediately generating the huge amount of traffic that larger companies can often get as soon as their Web sites go live, they're free to create a Web site that may initially be less-than-perfect, and then slowly expand and refine it. In sum, we suggest you think about your Web site as looking more like an electronic bulletin board than a software product.

Summary

When developing your content development strategy, it's often helpful to examine common goals for Web sites and the types of content appropriate to accomplish these goals. After examining what other companies have done, it's easier to determine the goals your company or organization will have for its own Web site. After you have established your goals, we believe that you'll be able to rapidly create and make your Web site available to visitors by taking a sort of bulletin-board approach to your Web site—placing whatever information you have up rather quickly, and then slowly refining your site.

In "Step 3: "Lay a Foundation," you learn how to acquire a domain name and choose an ISP to host your Web site, two tasks you need to accomplish before you can begin building your Web site.

Step 3

LAY A FOUNDATION

Featuring:

- Domain Name Background
- Why You Need Your Own Domain Name
- Choosing a Registrar
- Choosing a Web Hosting Service
- Signing Up for Service

Before you can begin constructing a Web site, you need to lay a foundation by acquiring a domain name and choosing a company to host your site. Because of how quickly domain names are being registered (and thus eliminated as potential names for your company or organization), it's important to take care of this step as soon as possible.

TIP *This is a good time to assess who will work on your Web site and to assemble everyone involved. If you have any information technology professionals in your company or organization, they could be a big help in laying your Web site's foundation, as well as smoothing out the creation process. Artistic employees can often help determine what works visually for the Web site, or create unique graphics for your site as necessary. Others can prove invaluable for their knowledge of what content is available for use on the Web site or for their ideas on what would be appropriate content to add to the site.*

Domain Name Background

Although it is not absolutely necessary to understand what domain names are and how they work, a little background helps to make the process of acquiring a domain name and setting it up with your Web host easier and more logical. Fortunately, as a business user, there are only three essential pieces of information you'll want to understand: IP addresses, DNS, and domain hierarchy.

NOTE *To follow this discussion, you'll find it helpful to first understand the technical details of how the Internet works. If you don't already possess this information, you may want to quickly review "Step 1: Learn the Logic."*

IP Address

Computers on the Internet use an Internet protocol (IP) address to identify the precise location of the computer. An IP address makes it possible for people and programs to find the computer on the Internet. Without an IP address, a computer can't communicate on the Internet.

Unfortunately, IP addresses are rather cumbersome. An IP address consists of four sets of three numbers, for example, 169.254.255.254, making it difficult to remember.

DNS

Because of the user-unfriendly nature of IP addresses, a service was created to allow people to access Internet computers using names instead of long strings of numbers. This service is called the Domain Name Service (DNS). What the DNS service does, essentially, is translate the name you use to identify an Internet resource, such as a Web site, to the IP address that the network actually uses to locate the Internet resource. The DNS service is performed by a computer called a DNS server.

If you type *www.microsoft.com* in the Address box of a Web browser, for example, your computer asks your ISP's DNS server for Microsoft's IP address. The DNS server looks up the IP address and sends it back. Your computer then uses the IP address that it received to retrieve the Web page. This process is illustrated in Figure 3-1.

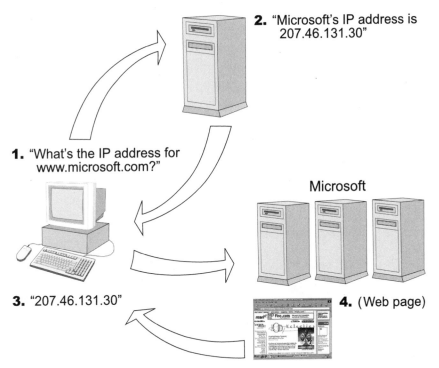

2. "Microsoft's IP address is 207.46.131.30"

1. "What's the IP address for www.microsoft.com?"

Microsoft

3. "207.46.131.30"

4. (Web page)

Figure 3-1 What happens when you request a Web page from *www.microsoft.com*.

Domain Hierarchy

Domain names themselves are hierarchical and are read in blocks from right to left, with each dot indicating the next layer of hierarchy. Thus, the three letters at the end (right side) of the domain name make up the top-level domain—in the case of most businesses, *.com*.

Past the top-level domain (*.com*) is the domain name itself, for example *microsoft*. To the left of the domain name is the host name, or subdomain, that is, the name of a specific computer or a child domain. Usually this is the *www* host name, the traditional host name of a Web server. Figure 3-2 shows this hierarchy for Microsoft's domain name.

NOTE   *A company can also have multiple subdomains within its domain. For example, besides* www.microsoft.com, *Microsoft also has* support.microsoft.com *(for product support) and* search.microsoft.com *(for searching Microsoft's Web site) subdomains.*

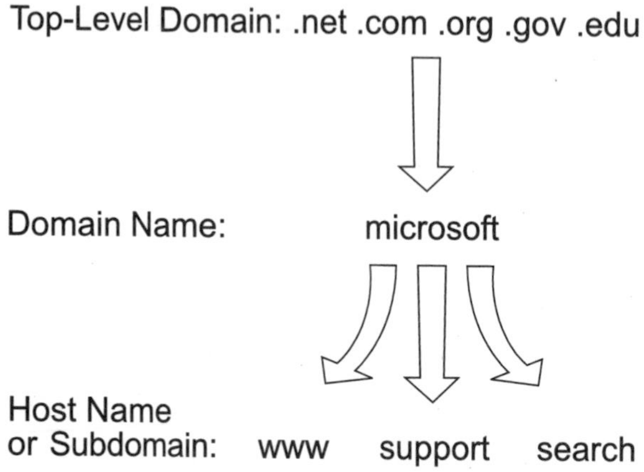

Top-Level Domain: .net .com .org .gov .edu

Domain Name: microsoft

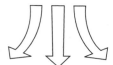

Host Name
or Subdomain: www   support   search

Figure 3-2   The hierarchy of Microsoft's domain name.

NOTE   *In reality, a single Web server may host multiple domains (as is typical with Web hosting companies) or multiple Web servers may host the same domain and appear as the same host (as is typical with very high-volume Web sites that would overload a single server—for example, www.microsoft.com). While these two exceptions are more the norm on the Internet itself, on corporate intranets (private networks using Web servers and the TCP/IP protocol), each computer has its own host name and normally only one.*

Why You Need Your Own Domain Name

When creating your Web site, you don't *have* to acquire your own domain name. You *can* use the domain name of your Web hosting company to save money, since most ISPs provide free Web hosting under their domain names. Thus your Web site's address would be something like *www.yourisp.com/~yourcompany*, where *yourisp* is the name of your ISP and *yourcompany* is the name of your company.

You typically don't want to do this, however. First, this approach confuses Web visitors about your firm's identity. This approach usually creates awkward URLs, or addresses. And this approach makes it more difficult to move from one ISP to another.

Getting your own domain name—such as *www.yourcompany.com*—requires only a bit more work, and the extra cost is usually modest. You may pay $15 to $35 a year for the name and perhaps an extra $10 a month for Web hosting.

Your own domain name also gives you insurance in case you need to or want to switch Web hosting companies. If you don't have your own domain name, your Web site address (and most likely your e-mail addresses, too) will change if you change Web hosts. When you have your own domain name, the only thing you need to change are some hidden settings maintained by the registrar from whom you purchased the domain name. Your Web site address and e-mail address continue to work as before.

Picking a Domain Name

Picking a domain name is a small step in the creation of a company or organization's Web site, but in many cases your domain name is at least as important as the name of your organization. Your domain name identifies your Web site, and by extension, your business or organization.

Accordingly, there are several points to consider when picking a domain name. First of all, you want your domain name to be descriptive of your company or organization. Your first choice is your business's name, but in some instances you might choose a domain name that's based on your business's purpose instead. For example, it might be much better for a business named Vladimir Berkowitz Faucets, Inc. to select the *www.greatfaucets.com* domain name instead of *www.vladamirberkowitzfaucets.com*.

If at all possible, your domain name should be easy to remember and spell. While a name like *www.rhythm.com* may be short and easy to remember, some people will have trouble spelling "rhythm," potentially eliminating a large number of visitors. Perhaps something like *www.beat.com* would be a better choice.

Short domain names are far preferable to long ones, although not if the name is difficult to remember. This is particularly important since most of the desirable short domain names have already been taken. It may be tempting to abbreviate your domain name to shorten it, but do this only if the abbreviation doesn't make the name harder to remember.

NOTE   *Barnes and Noble provides a good example of abbreviating a domain name. Its abbreviation is only two letters,* www.bn.com, *which for many people is easier to remember than* www.barnesandnoble.com. *However, Barnes and Noble provides visitors with the ability to use either domain name to access its site, allowing visitors to use whichever name they can remember. In other words, you can get to the Barnes and Noble Web site by using either* www.bn.com *or* www.barnesandnoble.com.

Multiple domain names may be something you want to consider, too. They increase the likelihood that people will find you, and cost only $15 to $35 per year more per domain name (although your Web host will probably charge a one-time setup fee of $30 or so). Multiple domain names also prevent others from skimming visitors from your Web site by choosing a similar domain name. Extra domain names to consider purchasing include the following:

- Your company or organization name if you picked a more descriptive domain name to use as your primary domain name.

- Former names of the company or organization.

- Common misspellings of your domain name.

- Longer versions of your domain name, or an abbreviated version of your domain name.

- The same domain name using a different top-level domain. For example, if you registered the *www.mycompany.com* domain name, you might want to also register *www.mycompany.org* or *.net* if you want to prevent others from taking those names.

Picking a Top-Level Domain

Besides the domain name itself, your company or organization also needs to choose which top-level domain to use, such as *.com* or *.net* or *.org*.

By far the most popular top-level domain to use is *.com*. Since this is the top-level domain most people will look under first, we recommend that businesses look for a *.com* domain name.

The *.net* domain is more appropriate for ISPs, Web hosting companies, and other Internet technologies companies.

Nonprofit organizations should probably use the *.org* top-level domain, although depending on the nature of the organization you might also consider registering your domain name with a *.com* top-level domain.

Once your organization has come up with some ideas for domain names, it's time to check for their availability. Because a large number of domain names are registered every day, make a list of alternate domain names in case the domain name you want is already taken. Then either go to any registrar's Web site (Network Solutions is the original, and most expensive, registrar *www.networksolutions.com*) or go to *www.betterwhois.com* and enter your domain name idea in the box provided, as shown in Figure 3-3.

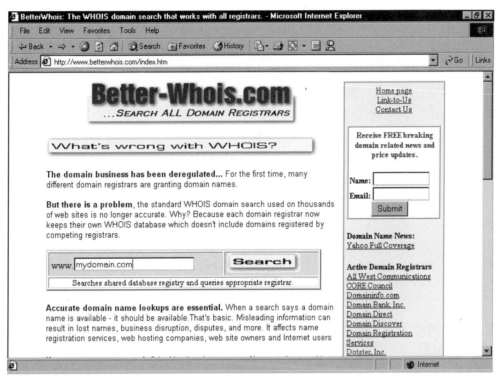

Figure 3-3   Checking out a potential domain name at the *www.betterwhois.com* Web site.

TIP   *If it's absolutely necessary for your company or organization to get a great domain name and all of your top choices are taken, you can look into after-market domain names. These are domain names that were already purchased and are now being resold for a usually obnoxious price. If you think it might be worth the added cost and effort, a list of aftermarket domain name brokers is available on* www.dnresources.com.

Valid Domain Names

While most companies will naturally choose a valid domain name, there are a few restrictions on domain names to keep in mind. Domain names are case insensitive, so don't spend time thinking about what letters to capitalize. Also, you can use only letters and the hyphen character—but a hyphen can't start or finish a domain name. Lastly, the domain name can be a maximum of 63 characters long, not including the *www.* and the top-level domain (*.com*, *.net* or *.org*).

Try to keep your domain names as short as possible. The average adult can remember at most seven or eight "chunks" of information, which can be letters, numbers, or words. If you choose a domain name longer than about five or six words (with maybe a chunk or two used up by the www and .com), people aren't going to be able to remember your domain name long enough to write it down, let alone remember it the next time they're in front of a computer.

Domain Name Disputes

In general, if another company or individual takes the domain name you wanted, use one of the alternate domain names your company or organization chose. However, if the other company or individual took the domain name specifically to negatively affect your company, you may be able to dispute their domain name registration.

In order to dispute a domain name registration, your company or organization needs to give evidence that all three of the following conditions were met:

- The domain name in question is identical or confusingly similar to a trademark or service mark to which your company or organization has legal rights.

- The current owner of the domain name has no rights or legitimate interests in the domain name.

- The domain name was registered and used in bad faith (to somehow take advantage of the domain name by either selling it for a profit, preventing the legitimate company or organization from acquiring it and/or disrupting their business, or by using it to take advantage of confused visitors going to the wrong site).

If you feel that your company or organization has a legitimate dispute on a domain name and you want to take action, refer to the Internet Corporation for Assigned Names and Numbers Web site at *www.icann.org*.

When your ideal domain name is already taken, it's often by another company with a similar name but a different business. This typically means that you can't dispute the domain name. However, depending on the domain name you end up choosing and the willingness of the other company, you may be able to arrange a link exchange to help both companies' visitors find the correct site. Usually each company places a small link to the other company's Web site on their home page, enabling lost visitors to find the correct Web site.

Choosing a Registrar

In order to use a domain name, you need to purchase it from an accredited Internet domain name registrar. In the past, this meant Internic—now called Network Solutions *(www.networksolutions.com)*. However, the Network Solutions lock on domain name registrations is over, and a multitude of companies can now sell you domain names.

Generally, the easiest way to set up a domain name is to let your Web hosting company set it up for you. This is usually done when you sign up for Web site hosting, and it saves you the work of transferring your domain name from an independent registrar to your Web hosting company (see the "Signing Up for Service" section later in this step). The only downside is that this service is usually provided through Network Solutions, which is the most expensive registrar.

If you are willing to expend a slightly larger amount of time and effort in acquiring a domain name, you can get one yourself from another registrar. Network Solutions charges $70 for two years, but other registrars are available with cheaper prices. Some even offer free domain name registration if you use the registrar as your Web hosting company. Besides the additional time required to find a registrar, you'll also need to transfer your new domain to your Web hosting company, which takes a bit more time and effort (see the "Signing Up for Service" section later in this step). For a current listing of available registrars, go to the Domain Name Resources Web site at *www.dnresources.com*.

Choosing a Web Hosting Service

Choosing a company to host your Web site can be a bewildering experience. With thousands of Web hosting companies, each usually offering several different hosting plans, it takes knowledge and a certain amount of patience to choose a Web hosting company.

In general, however, you want to look at two issues. The first issue is which features the company offers for its price. The reliability and quality of the company also need to be established, and while this is notoriously difficult to ascertain, we can give you some pointers to look for in the following sections. The second issue is whether to choose a local Web hosting company or a national one.

Comparing Host Features

Web hosting companies offer numerous features—most described with hard-to-decipher technical jargon. Therefore, the following paragraphs provide you with summary descriptions of the features that are often available, along with information you can use to determine which ones are relevant for your firm or organization.

Virtual Domains/Domain Hosting

In order to use your own domain name *(www.yourcompany.com)*, the Web hosting company needs to support virtual domains or domain hosting (different companies use different terms). Usually, this capability is a basic feature of "business" hosting plans, but often it isn't a feature of most "personal" hosting plans; hence, the business vs. personal distinction (personal Web sites don't usually need their own domain names).

The bottom line is that the Web hosting company you choose must support virtual domains or domain hosting if you want to be able to use your own domain name (which you do).

FrontPage 2000 Server Extensions

If you plan on using FrontPage to create and manage your Web site—and you probably do if you're reading this book—then you want your Web hosting company to support FrontPage Server Extensions.

FrontPage Server Extensions allow you to easily publish your Web site without using cumbersome tools, such as FTP or the Microsoft Web Publishing Wizard. They also provide server-based tools that can be indispensable when creating a Web site for an organization, such as the support for forms, discussion groups, and Web site search capability.

NOTE   *In the absence of FrontPage 2000 Server Extensions, you need to use tools like CGI scripts to provide components such as Web forms. CGI scripts, however, require technology know-how beyond the scope of this book.*

Disk Space Allotment

Many organizations will find that the amount of disk space allotted to their Web site isn't a crucial factor in the decision of which company to use for Web hosting. Most companies and organizations' Web sites are rather small, and generally don't have trouble fitting comfortably in the 25MB of Web space provided by even the most barebones Web hosting plans you might look at.

If you plan on having a large number of images, audio, or video files on your Web site, however, disk space allotment becomes an important issue. If this could be the case, you may want to opt for a hosting plan that offers 100MB, 200MB, or unlimited disk space.

Database Support and Active Server Pages

If your firm or organization wants to use a database on your Web site and dynamically create pages based on data from the database (this is what Active Server Pages are), your Web hosting company needs to support both databases and Active Server Pages.

Setting up a database on your Web site is a difficult task, although it is something that your company or organization could hire a consultant to do, after which you could then maintain it rather easily in-house. If you think that your company may want to set up a database on your Web site for information retrieval, online ordering, or some other purpose, make sure that your hosting plan supports Active Server Pages and database integration with FrontPage 2000.

E-Mail Accounts and Aliases

Most Web hosting companies will provide your company or organization with e-mail accounts using your domain name for free with your Web hosting. For most organizations this is a pretty important feature.

However, different hosting plans offer different numbers of e-mail accounts (though most offer additional accounts for a charge). So, in general, pick a hosting plan or company that provides the number of e-mail accounts you need included in the price, since adding extra mail accounts can quickly increase the monthly cost of your Web site.

Besides e-mail accounts, most hosting plans also offer e-mail aliases. An e-mail alias works like a sort of virtual e-mail address that forwards received mail to another address. For example, you could set up an info@yourcompany.com alias that forwards all mail received by that e-mail address to gerendj@hotmail.com. Most Web hosting plans provide either a very large number of aliases or an unlimited number. This allows you to create as many e-mail addresses using your domain name as you want (even if you have a limited number of real e-mail accounts)—provided the people you're creating addresses for already have at least one e-mail account elsewhere that they can use.

NOTE *E-mail accounts can be accessed in several ways. The most common way is to use a POP server in which all mail is downloaded from the server into your mail program, such as Microsoft Outlook, Outlook Express, or Qualcomm Eudora. A newer method that allows messages to be stored on the mail server (and thus remain accessible from multiple locations) is IMAP, which can also be used with most popular e-mail programs (although Outlook Express can't create message rules for IMAP accounts). Some Web hosting companies also provide Web-based e-mail account access (in addition to POP or IMAP access), allowing you to check your e-mail from any Web browser when away from your own computer. If your company or organization has users who frequently use multiple computers or travel often, consider using IMAP e-mail accounts or a Web hosting company that provides Web-based e-mail account access.*

Subdomains

Some Web hosting companies allow you to create subdomains for your Web site, such as *support.yourcompany.com* or *events.yourcompany.com*. This isn't an important feature for most smaller companies and organizations. In fact, you should avoid needlessly creating subdomains, since the main reason to create a subdomain is to make it easier for people to go directly to a specific part of your Web site—something which is generally better done with a link on your home page.

If your company has separate divisions that want their own Web sites, however, subdomains are a cost-effective solution, since you can have as many subdomains as your Web host allows without having to pay any additional registration fees (because you're still using only one domain name). Subdomains are administered and created separately, which can be highly desirable for divisions of your company that want their own autonomy, but it is an added burden on your Web site staff if this autonomy isn't needed.

Mailing Lists, List Servers, and Majordomo

Depending on your business or organization, you may want to start an e-mail mailing list that you can use to send mass mailings to all people subscribed to the list. This is very useful for sending out information about upcoming events, specials, or tips.

A number of methods exist for creating mailing lists, but if your organization thinks this might be a desirable capability, consider finding a Web hosting company that includes some sort of mailing list capability at little or no extra cost. Some of the more common programs used for mailing lists are the Majordomo programs, Listserv, and Petidomo.

NOTE *For more information on dealing with mailing lists, see "Step 8: Deploy Your Web Site."*

Data Transfer Limitations

Some Web hosting companies have a limit as to how much data can be transferred per month. Every time someone views a page on your Web site or downloads a file, they're transferring data from your Web site. Similarly, when you upload new pages or files to your Web site, you're also transferring data. If your Web site goes above this limit (due to lots of visitors or large file downloads), you're charged extra.

Although most Web sites don't generate a lot of data transfers even when they're busy, if you anticipate having a popular Web site with lots of images, audio/video, or downloadable files, you may want to opt for a Web hosting service that doesn't have a data transfer limit.

SSL (Security)

Secure Sockets Layer (SSL) is a way of encrypting data that is transferred to and from a Web site, and it is typically used for Web stores that process credit card transactions. As such, it is an important feature if your organization plans to set up an online store, although you'll probably need to hire outside help for this. Otherwise, the feature isn't necessary.

Technical Support

All Web hosting companies provide technical support for any problems with publishing your Web site, Web site availability, e-mail, and so forth. However, the type, quality, and availability of this support vary. Not all companies provide toll-free technical support phone numbers; not all companies provide 24-hour, 7-day-a-week (24/7) technical support.

NOTE *The toll-free number might be important to you, but the always-available technical support might not be if there isn't going to be anyone working on or checking your Web site after hours.*

Another support option that is becoming increasingly popular is Web-based technical support. This allows visitors to conduct a live chat with a technical support person over your Internet connection, and it is handy for people who don't want to wait on hold. (You might have to wait online, but many people find it easier to get work done while they are waiting this way.)

Web Server Speed

The speed of a Web server is fairly difficult to ascertain from reading promotional material on a company's Web site. In fact, it's probably impossible, which is unfortunate because Web server speed is important.

Reading reviews of hosting companies can be helpful, but difficult to find. You can ask companies about their Web hosting speed, but in our experience people often tell you the same thing—they're fast enough. Nevertheless, to be thorough, you probably want to check on several things.

One of the first questions you want to ask is, how much bandwidth is available? A Web server running off a T1 connection may saturate the connection during busy times or if it is hosting too many Web sites. When the connection is fully utilized, Web site performance suffers. Table 3-1 summarizes the different connection speeds commonly used for Web servers.

CONNECTION TYPE	BANDWIDTH
T1	1.544Mbps
T3	45Mbps
T4	259.4Mbps
DS1	3.088Mbps
DS2	6.176Mbps
DS3	45Mbps
OC1	51.84Mbps
OC2	103.68Mbps
OCn	n*51.84Mbps

Table 3-1   Web server Internet connections and their associated bandwidths.

The second important question to ask is, how many sites is a Web server hosting? A super-fast Internet connection on an extremely powerful Web server doesn't mean your Web site is going to be fast if there are too many other Web sites hosted by the same Web server. Similarly, if too many users share the Internet connection's bandwidth, performance will suffer. Many Web hosting companies also act as ISPs and share the available bandwidth with both dial-up and DSL customers as well as their Web servers.

A third important question to ask is, how fast is their server? While Web hosting isn't typically a processor-intensive application, hosting many sites or hosting very busy sites can strain a server. Once again it's hard to make a direct comparison, since the necessary speed of a server depends directly on the number and business of the Web sites it's hosting. In general though, Web servers running powerful (sometimes multiple) processors provide extra speed. Similarly, Web servers that use a RAID for storage (a RAID is a collection of hard drives that is treated as one drive by the operating system) also provide extra speed and reliability.

Web Server Reliability

Even more important than Web server speed is the reliability of the server. Although people can still view a Web site on an overburdened Web server (albeit at a slower speed), when a server goes down, nobody can view the sites hosted by that server.

To assess Web server reliability, most people rely on the uptime percentage, which is something that can easily be measured. Most organizations aim for 99.9 percent uptime (roughly 9 hours of downtime a year).

To attain a good uptime percentage, reliable Web hosts use a variety of hardware and software to decrease the potential for downtime. Web servers should use a hardware RAID for storage, protecting your data in case a hard drive dies. The hosting company should also perform routine tape backups of all data, as well as keep its Web servers on UPS (Uninterruptible Power Supply) devices and possibly even have backup generators for major power trouble.

In terms of software, the Web servers should be running Windows 2000 Server with the latest service pack and hotfixes (fixes provided in between service packs) if you're going to use (or think you're going to use) FrontPage Server Extensions. Alternatively, many Web hosting companies prefer to run some form of Unix, which can be even more reliable, but in general, FrontPage Server Extensions are more stable under Windows 2000 than Unix.

NOTE *Some Web hosting companies may still be running their Web servers on Windows NT 4 Server with the latest service pack. While this isn't a bad thing (Windows NT 4 is a very reliable operating system), Windows 2000 Server is even more reliable and easier to keep running. It's not a major issue, but in general it's preferable for a Web server to be running under Windows 2000 than Windows NT 4.*

Local vs. National Web Hosting

One important decision that can be difficult to make is whether your organization should use a local or out-of-state Web hosting company.

Using a local company can be advantageous if you need consulting work done on your Web site in addition to Web hosting, since most local Web hosting companies also do Web site consulting work as well. While national companies can also consult or work on your Web site, there's often no substitute for meeting in person with a consultant and discussing what needs to be done. When that consultant happens to work for your Web hosting company, he or she is often more effective in working on your site (at least if database integration or electronic commerce is involved).

When you use a local company, there's also an additional form of action that you can take when you have problems or questions about your Web site—you can go down and knock on the door. If you're a more face-to-face type of person, this can be highly desirable, but most companies will find phone and online support perfectly adequate.

Using a local Web hosting company also supports your local economy. Some organizations—both for-profit firms and nonprofit organizations—want to support their local communities in a variety of ways, and this can be one of those ways.

However, local Web hosting companies usually cost more and provide fewer features than national companies. This is what nationwide competition does for you—it allows you to pick the best mix of price and features for your company from a pool of thousands of Web hosting companies. It's most unlikely that the best value will happen to be your local Web hosting firm. Local companies also often lack some of the features that out-of-town companies offer, such as 24/7 technical support, large numbers of e-mail addresses, large amounts of disk space, and the ability to use subdomains.

Where to Find a Web Hosting Company

Even armed with good selection criteria, you'll still need to locate prospective Web hosting companies. And with the thousands of Web hosting companies that you can choose from, narrowing your list of candidates to a reasonable number can be a time-consuming and difficult process. Several useful resources exist, however, to point you in the right direction.

TIP   *Choosing a Web hosting company isn't a permanent decision. You can easily switch companies at almost any time (although you might choose to sign up for a one-year contract to avoid setup fees). So don't waste too much time trying to find "the one"—take a little time, find one you like, and then try it out. If you later locate a better one, switch when your contract is up.*

Microsoft's Locate A Web Presence Provider Web Site

Located at *www.microsoftwpp.com* (shown in Figure 3-4), the Microsoft Locate A Web Presence Provider Web site allows you to perform a search for a Web hosting company that is a Microsoft registered host for FrontPage Web sites. This is probably the best place to search for a Web hosting company if you plan on using FrontPage 2000 to build your Web site.

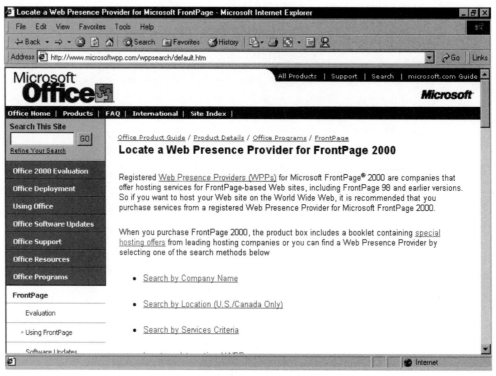

Figure 3-4   Microsoft's Locate A Web Presence Provider Web site.

DN Resources

The *www.dnresources.com* Web site has a special Hosting section (shown in Figure 3-5) that provides a list of Web sites that provide a list of Web hosting companies. It's a little confusing, since each Web site listed shows a somewhat different list of Web hosting companies, not all of which adequately support FrontPage 2000 Web sites. However, it can still be a good place to come up with companies to possibly host your site.

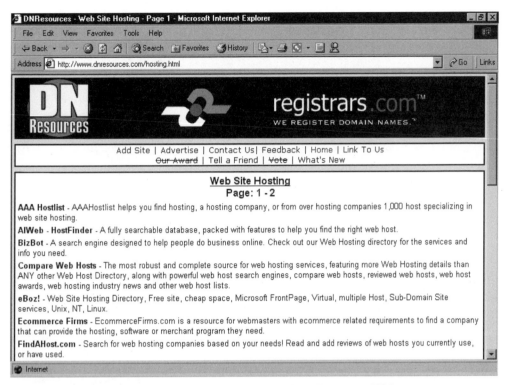

Figure 3-5 The Web Site Hosting section of the DN Resources Web site.

Local Computer Papers

If you're looking for a local Web hosting company, check out any local computer papers or the technology section of your local paper for ads from local companies. You can also check the Yellow Pages under Internet.

Signing Up for Service

After deciding on a domain name, locating a Web hosting company, and selecting the appropriate hosting plan, you need to sign up for the actual service. While the details of the signup process are different for every company, the basic steps are going to be nearly identical no matter what company you use.

1. Locate your Web hosting company.

Find the Web hosting company you want to use and go to its Web site. More information on locating Web hosting companies is given in the previous section.

2. Find the plan you want and start the signup process.

Locate the hosting plan that is best suited to your company or organization on the Web hosting company's Web site. This is typically the cheapest one that offers all the features you need. Look for the "Business" plans. Once you've found the best plan for your company or organization, click Order Now or a similar link.

TIP *If you're uncertain about some of the questions on the signup forms or prefer to talk to a person, call the Web hosting company—it's just as easy to sign up for Web hosting service over the phone.*

3. Get your domain name.

This is typically the first step of the hosting company's signup process (as shown in Figure 3-6). To allow the Web hosting company to take care of the domain name registration, indicate that this is a new domain and enter the domain name you want in the box provided. If you already have a domain, specify that you already have a domain or that you want to transfer a domain, and then enter the domain name in the box provided. If you want to get your domain name from a registrar other than Network Solutions, go to the registrar's site and purchase the domain name, and then come back and enter it on the Web hosting company's signup form.

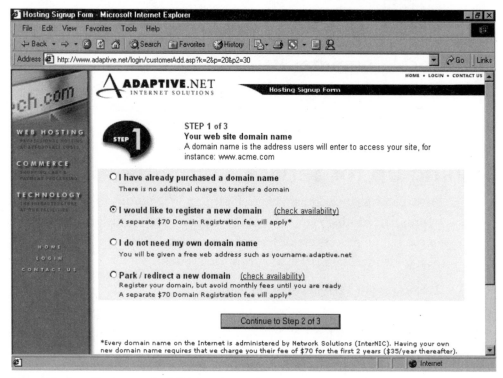

Figure 3-6 Signing up for Web hosting and registering a new domain name.

NOTE *Most Web hosting companies use Network Solutions for registering domain names, which charges $70 to register your domain name for two years. If you already have a domain name or want to save money by using a different registrar, make sure to choose the Transfer Existing Domain or similar option.*

4. Provide an e-mail address and password.

Enter the e-mail address that you want to use to receive information about your new Web site, as shown in Figure 3-7. Enter a password for your Web site also—preferably a somewhat long one that only you or your Web site administrator will know.

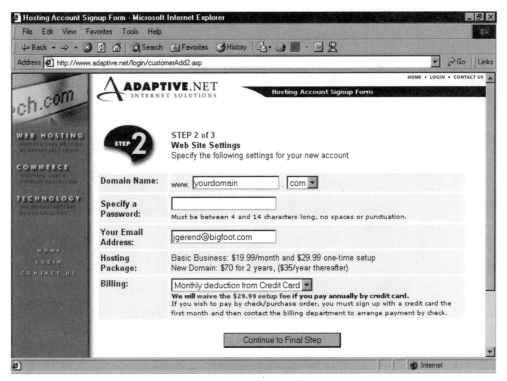

Figure 3-7 Entering an e-mail address, Web site password, and domain name.

TIP   *Keep your Web site's password in a secure location and give it only to employees who will administer the Web site. When employees who know the password leave your organization, change the password.*

5. Fill out user and billing information.

Verify your domain name and enter your credit card and billing information in the last step of the Web hosting signup form, as shown in Figure 3-8.

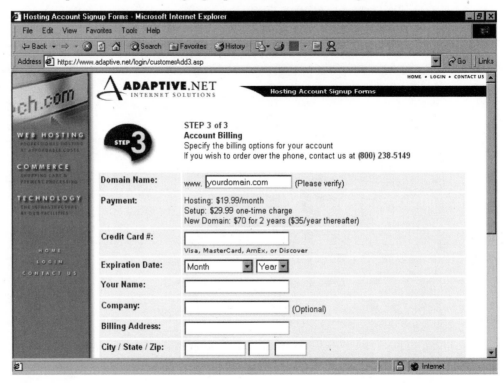

Figure 3-8   The Web hosting signup form.

6. Transfer your domain name (if registered separately).

If you are transferring a domain name from another Web hosting company (or if you purchased a domain name from another registrar), go to your registrar's Web site, sign in, and change the name servers to those provided by your new Web hosting company. This typically involves clicking one or more Modify Domains links, as shown in Figure 3-9, then entering the primary and secondary name servers' IP addresses and names (your Web hosting company will give you these) in the boxes provided, as shown in Figure 3-10. Doing this instructs the domain name registrar where to send visitors looking for your Web site.

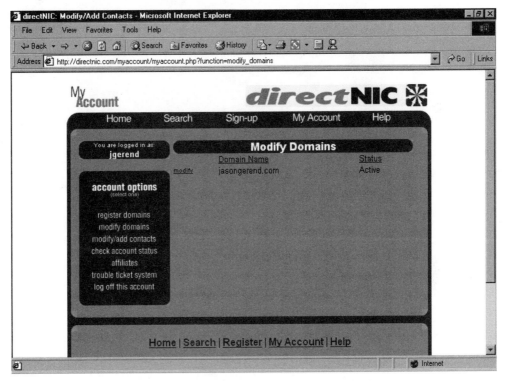

Figure 3-9   The Modify Domains section of a domain name registrar.

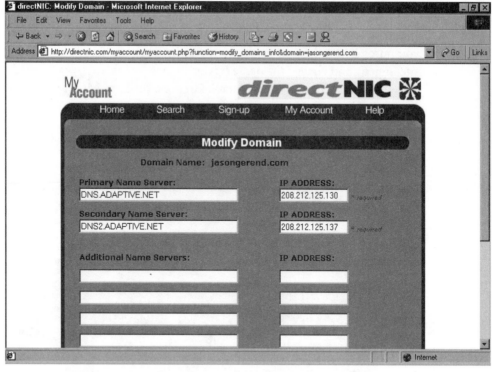

Figure 3-10 Entering your Web hosting company's name servers.

NOTE *Once you've set up your Web hosting account, you'll need to set up any e-mail accounts you want to use in a separate procedure. You should at the very least create info@yourdomain.com and webmaster@yourdomain.com accounts or aliases to handle general information questions and comments or problems with the Web site. This is typically done by logging onto your Web hosting company's Web site and adding any e-mail accounts and aliases you want. Check with your Web hosting company for more information on the exact procedure. It varies with each company.*

Summary

After selecting a domain name and signing up for Web hosting service, you're ready to assemble your content in preparation for constructing your Web site. "Step 4: Collect and Organize Your Content" gives you some solid suggestions that you can use to help your company or organization collect, create, and organize content for your Web site.

Step 4

COLLECT AND ORGANIZE YOUR CONTENT

Featuring:

- Determining What Needs to Be Done

- Creating a Central Location for Content

- Establishing a File Naming Convention

- Collecting Existing Digital Content

- Creating New Digital Content

- Organizing Content and Planning Your Web Site

Once you've completed the initial steps in the process of creating a Web site, it's time to actually round up your content and create the Web site itself. While it may be tempting to jump right in and immediately start creating pages, take time to collect and create your content first, organize it into a logical structure, and *then* create your Web pages. Doing so will yield a Web site that makes more sense, conveys the information you want, is easier to use—basically a Web site that is more effective.

The process of organizing and planning a Web site can be as simple or as complex as you desire. Whole businesses exist solely to help companies plan Web sites, and conversely, simple Web sites can be created with no prior planning or organization. However, the majority of organizations will find that the optimal path lies somewhere in between these two extremes.

Even though we recommend spending a little time gathering and organizing your content before creating your Web site, it is appropriate to create a simple Web page (even something as simple as a glorified Yellow Pages listing) and post it to your Web site in the interim.

Determining What Needs to Be Done

Many companies find it helpful to sit down with everyone involved in creating the Web site and develop a game plan that your organization can use to get started efficiently. Briefly walking through the items on the following list can help you assign tasks and increase the quality of the content that you ultimately collect.

- Where should content be stored? All Web site content should ideally be moved or copied to a central location while the Web site is being constructed. Decide on what network disk or computer the content should be stored, and inform everyone involved with the project of this location.

- Do you have existing digital content? What kind of existing content does your company or organization have that's already in digital (computer readable) form and is appropriate to use for your Web site? An exhaustive inventory isn't necessary. Just quickly identify the kinds of content that you already have and determine what needs to be done in order to prepare it for use on your Web site.

- What new content needs to be created? Briefly identify the kinds of content that needs to be created from scratch or imported into the computer (through scanning, retyping, or importing from a digital camera), and then establish how the content will be created.

- How should the content be structured? Sketch a rough outline of how your Web site should be organized. Creating this preliminary outline may help find and create content that fits with the purpose and design of your Web site. Don't stick too firmly to your preliminary design, because as content is created and collected you'll probably want to make some changes. When you create the Web site, you'll find even more changes to make.

TIP *As you collect, create, and organize content for your Web site, it's possible that your idea about the site's purpose will change. If need be, flip back to "Step 3: Lay a Foundation," and refine your Web site's new purpose.*

Creating a Central Location for Content

Repeatedly searching for content in a number of different locations not only decreases productivity but also increases the chance that important content will get misplaced or duplicated on your Web site.

When you actually create a Web site in FrontPage, FrontPage creates a new folder called a FrontPage web that it uses to store the Web site. However, because all files stored in the FrontPage web will eventually get published to your Web server (and made available on the Internet), it makes sense to have a completely separate folder in which to store content before it gets added to the Web site, as shown in Figure 4-1. Think of it as a staging area for content—anything that your company considers potential content can be placed in this separate folder to be evaluated and added to the Web site as appropriate.

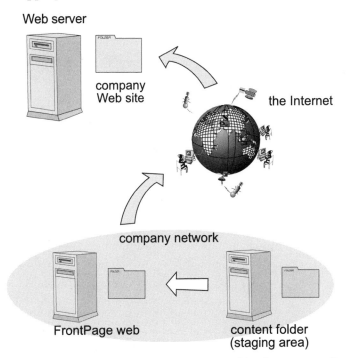

Figure 4-1   Where Web content is stored in the process of creating Web pages.

TIP   *You may find that your organization doesn't need a central content folder, perhaps because all your content is quickly integrated into the Web site or because it is easy to locate without having to centralize it. If this is the case, when we suggest looking in or placing content in your central content folder, just go to the source of your content instead.*

Before you create a folder in which to store your potential Web content, first decide on an appropriate computer or network disk. It's ideal to use a network disk that is both backed up regularly and uses some method of protecting against hard disk failure (such as a Redundant Array of Independent Disks, or RAID). It's also preferable to use a Windows 2000 or Windows NT partition formatted using the NTFS file system, which provides additional security features. However, if your company or organization doesn't have these resources, simply choose the most convenient computer or network disk.

The central content folder could be located on the same computer or network disk as the FrontPage web (which you'll probably want to place on a local computer running a Web server program such as Internet Information Server, which comes with Windows 2000, and Windows NT 4), or in a completely different location.

After you've decided on a location, create the folder by following these steps:

1. **Launch Windows Explorer.**

   Click the Start button, choose Programs, and then click Windows Explorer. (If you're using Windows 2000, click the Start button, choose Programs, choose Accessories, and then click Windows Explorer.)

2. **Navigate to the location where you want to create the folder.**

   In the Folders pane on the left of the Windows Explorer window, click the plus sign next to the location where you want to store the content folder to expand the location's subfolders. For example, click the plus sign next to My Computer to view the local hard drives in your system (and any network disks that are mapped to a drive letter), as shown in Figure 4-2.

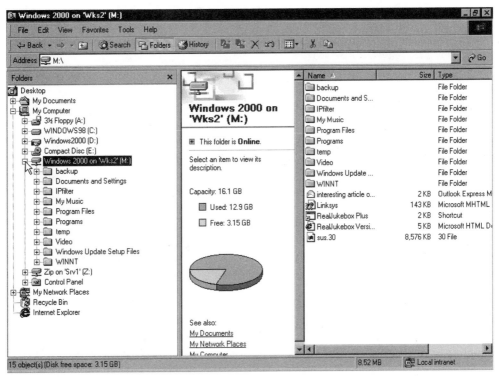

Figure 4-2 Navigating to the desired content folder location using Windows Explorer.

3. Create a new folder.

While viewing the drive or folder where you want to store your content, right-click a blank area of the right pane, choose New from the shortcut menu, and then choose Folder from the submenu, as shown in Figure 4-3.

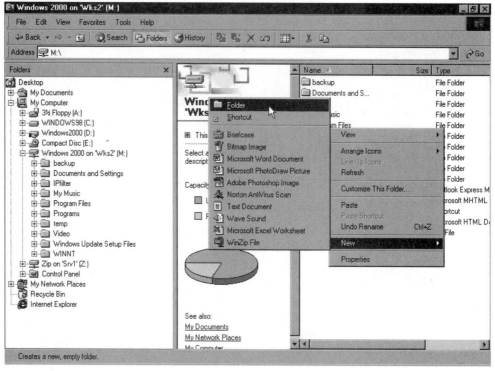

Figure 4-3 Creating a new folder using Windows Explorer.

4. Enter a name for the folder.

When you create a new folder, the folder name is automatically highlighted. Enter the name you want for the folder, and then click anywhere onscreen to save the name. If you make a mistake, right-click the folder and choose Rename from the shortcut menu.

Establishing a File Naming Convention

Before you start collecting or creating content for your company or organization's Web site, it's important to establish a file naming convention. This step makes it easier to identify files and work with them.

There are differing views as to what makes good file naming conventions, but consistency is paramount. Create some rules that work for your Web site, and stick to them. Here are some recommendations:

- Unix Web servers don't like spaces in filenames and handle capitalization differently than do Windows Web servers. To accommodate this, name your files using all lowercase letters, and instead of using spaces, use the underscore character or simply run words together, for example, webpresentation1.htm or web_presentation1.htm. Even if you're using a Windows Web server now, this makes your Web site more flexible if in the future you decide to move to a Unix Web server.

- If your content is time-sensitive, such as newsletter copy, use a date in the filename, either at the beginning of the name or at the end.

- Images often come in large and small sizes (full size and thumbnail). FrontPage automatically appends _small to the end of an image when it creates thumbnail images, for example, product1_small.jpg. (FrontPage's Auto Thumbnail feature is discussed in "Step 5: Create Your Web Site.") If you plan on using FrontPage to create thumbnail images, use _small at the end of thumbnail images you create manually.

Collecting Existing Digital Content

When creating a Web site, it can be a bit daunting at first thinking about all the content that needs to be created. Fortunately, most companies and organizations already have a large amount of digital content that can be used on a Web site with only a minimal amount of work.

When we say digital content, what we mean is any content that can be opened in a computer. This includes data on hard drives, your local network, the Internet (though be careful about copyrights), floppy and Zip disks, CD-ROMS, and so forth.

To use existing digital content (which comes in many types), you first need to locate it, and if necessary, convert the content to an appropriate format for importing into FrontPage.

Types of Digital Content to Look For

Just about any kind of digital content your company or organization has can be adapted for use on the Web. The following list gives examples of some common types of content that your organization might have that would be suitable for publishing on your Web site. (This list is by no means comprehensive. Other data types can also be used, although depending on your applications, it might take a little work to get them into Web page format.)

- Word processor documents (.doc, .txt, .wpf): This can be a big reservoir of content, including materials such as project reports, manuals, company objectives, newsletters, and notices to customers created with a word processing program, such as Microsoft Word, AppleWorks, or WordPerfect.

- PowerPoint presentations (.ppt): If your company or organization has any presentations, lecture slides, or demos that it's created, they might be great additions to your Web site.

- Spreadsheet documents (.xls): Data that your company or organization has analyzed in a spreadsheet program, such as Microsoft Excel, might also be good content for your Web site, provided it relates to the site's purpose and target audience. This could include financial information for nonprofit companies, analyzed data from technical companies, or statistical data for tests that have been conducted.

- Digital images (.jpg, .gif, .png, .fpx): A staple of any Web site, digital images that your company has are potential content for your Web site. This includes company logos or graphics created for brochures.

- Flyers, brochures, or other computer-created content: Flyers and brochures that your company has stored in some sort of computer format (perhaps created using Microsoft Publisher or Adobe PageMaker) are also excellent sources of content for a Web site.

- E-mails: Although special care needs to be taken when using e-mail conversations on a Web site, e-mails can often be a rich source of content for a Web site. Special messages sent out to customers can be placed in a Web page for users who didn't receive the e-mail, customer questions and answers can be integrated into a Frequently Asked Questions page, or visitor comments can be placed on a Feedback page (usually with names removed).

- Existing Web pages: This might seem obvious, but if your company or organization already has Web pages it's created for one reason or another, you should probably evaluate how useful they'd be on your new Web site.

- Sound files and/or video files (.wav, .au, .mp3, .mpg, .avi, .mov): Sound and video files are usually very large and should generally be avoided on Web sites, but some companies or organizations will find audio and/or video files that would be perfect for their sites. However, extreme discretion should be used with these files because of their large size and the slow speed of most visitors' Internet connections.

Locating Existing Digital Content

Before you can use any existing digital content on your company or organization's Web site, you need to identify where it is located. This may or may not be so easy, depending on the company and the data.

To locate the data, either look for it manually on your hard drives or use the Search tool built into Windows.

Manually Looking for Content

If you have a good idea where your content is located, look for it manually by following these steps:

1. **Launch Windows Explorer.**

   Click the Start button, choose Programs, and then click Windows Explorer. (If you're using Windows 2000, click the Start button, choose Programs, choose Accessories, and then click Windows Explorer.)

2. **Navigate to the folder containing your content.**

   In the Folders pane on the left of the Windows Explorer window, click the plus sign next to the location where you want to look for subfolders. For example, click the plus sign next to My Computer to look for content stored on your computer, as shown in Figure 4-4.

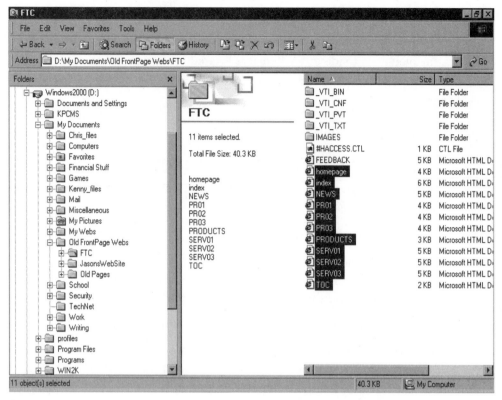

Figure 4-4   Locating content manually using Windows Explorer.

3. Copy the data to your central content folder.

To make it easier to find your content again, select the files you want to use and then choose the Edit menu's Copy command. Navigate to your content folder, select the folder or subfolder into which you want to copy the files, and then choose the Edit menu's Paste command.

TIP   *To select multiple contiguous files, select the first file, hold down the Shift key, and then select the last file you want to select. To select multiple files that aren't contiguous, hold down the Ctrl key while selecting each file.*

TIP   *To copy selected files, press the Ctrl and C keys simultaneously. To then paste the copied files, press the Ctrl and V keys simultaneously.*

Performing a Search for Content

If you don't know where your content is located or you want to do a thorough job of searching for potential content, use the Search tool built into Windows. This tool scours your drives looking for certain types of content. You'll need to specify what to look for, and you'll still need to look through the potentially large amount of content that is located, but this can be a great way to find content that's filed away in less-than-optimal locations.

To perform a search for content, follow these steps:

1. **Open the Search tool.**

   Click the Start button, choose Search, and then click For Files Or Folders. (If you're using Windows 98, click the Start button, choose Find, and then click Files Or Folders.)

2. **Enter the search criteria.**

   To search for all files of a specific file type, in the Search For Files Or Folders Named box, enter an asterisk, and then enter the three-letter extension of the file type you want to search for. For example, to search for Word documents, enter *.*doc*, as shown in Figure 4-5. This is usually the most effective way to search for files. A list of the more common file extensions is presented earlier in this step in the section "Types of Digital Content to Look For."

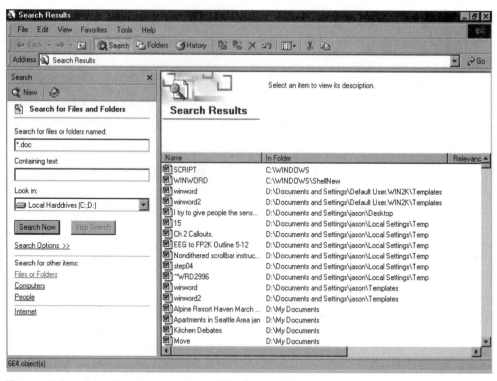

Figure 4-5   Searching for content in Windows 2000.

TIP   *You can use asterisks as wildcards when performing a search. The search program ignores the asterisk and returns any files that have the rest of the characters you specify in their filenames. For example, *.doc returns all files that have the .doc file extension; report.* returns all files named "report" no matter what their file extensions. You can also use asterisks inside filenames. For example, report*.doc returns any Word documents that begin with the characters "report."*

3. Specify where to search.

Use the Look In box to specify the drives or network computers in which to look for content. Select a drive from the list, or select Browse from the list to browse for a drive or network location.

4. Start the search.

Click the Search Now button to start searching for files that match the search criteria. If the search is taking too long, click the Stop Search button to discontinue the search.

5. Examine the search results.

Windows displays all the files it found that matched your search criteria in the Search Results pane on the right side of the window (see Figure 4-5). Scroll down the list to locate files that are potentially useful on your Web site. If you want to open a file in the search results, double-click it.

TIP   *If you uncover content that's stored in a location you haven't manually looked in, select the file in the Search Results window. This displays the file details at the top of the window, including the folder in which it's stored. Click the hyperlink labeled In Folder to look in that folder. Sometimes this uncovers additional files that did not show up in the search results that might be useful on your Web site.*

6. Copy the data to your central content folder.

To make it easier to find your content again, select the files you might want to use, and then choose the Edit menu's Copy command. Navigate to your content folder (as described earlier in this step in the section "Creating a Central Location for Content"), select the folder or subfolder into which you want to copy the files, and then choose the Edit menu's Paste command.

TIP   *Windows 2000 contains a powerful search feature called the Indexing Service. When turned on (it's off by default), the Indexing Service scans all supported data files (such as Microsoft Office documents) on your hard drives, making an index of information about each file's contents. After this index is created, you can perform searches for documents containing certain words or content. See the Windows 2000 Help system for more information.*

Converting Existing Data to an Appropriate Format

Although much of the content that you find you'll probably be able to import directly into FrontPage, some content will need to be converted into another file format in order to be used effectively on a Web site. FrontPage 2000 can convert a fairly large range of file formats into a Web page, as shown in Tables 4-1, 4-2, and 4-3.

EXTENSION	FILE FORMAT
.htm, .html, .htx, .otm, .asp	HTML files (Web pages)
.htt	Hypertext templates
.rtf	Rich Text Format (formatted text files)
.txt	Plain text files
.doc, .dot	Word documents (Word 97–2000)
.doc	Word documents (Word 6.0/95 for Windows and Macintosh)
.doc	Word documents (Word 6.0/95 Asian versions)
.doc	Word documents (Word 2.x for Windows)
.mcw	Word documents (Word for Macintosh 4.0–5.1)
.wk1, .wk3, .wk4	Lotus 1-2-3 files
.xls, .xlw	Excel worksheets
.wps	Microsoft Works 4.0 for Windows files
.wpd, .doc	WordPerfect 5.x–6.x documents
.wri	Windows Write documents

Table 4-1 Document formats FrontPage 2000 can import.

EXTENSION	FILE FORMAT
.gif	CompuServe Graphics Interchange Format (GIF) image
.jpg, .jpeg	Joint Photographic Experts Group (JPEG) image
.png	Portable Network Graphic (PNG) image
.bmp	Windows bitmap image
.tif, .tiff	Tagged Image Format (TIFF) image
.wmf	Windows Metafile image
.ras	Sun Raster image

EXTENSION	FILE FORMAT
.eps	PostScript file
.pcx	PCX image
.pcd	Kodak PhotoCD image
.tga	Targa image

Table 4-2   Image formats FrontPage 2000 can import.

EXTENSION	FILE FORMAT
.avi	Video For Windows video
.asf	Windows Media video
.ram, .ra	RealMedia audio or video
.wav	Windows wave sound file
.mid	MIDI sequencer sound file
.aif, .aifc, .aiff	AIFF sound file
.au, .snd	AU sound file

Table 4-3   Video and sound formats FrontPage 2000 can import.

FrontPage 2000 generally does a respectable job of importing content; however, most programs that support saving data in a Web page format (as an HTML file) do a better job with the conversion process. Some programs, such as Microsoft Office 2000, will actually export enhanced Web pages with a fair amount of interactivity (one example is the PowerPoint presentation exported to a Web page shown in Figure 4-6). If you're dealing with a complete presentation, spreadsheet chart, or any sort of content that you want to use in its entirety with little or no changes, using the native program's Save As Web Page feature (or equivalent feature) usually yields the most professional-looking results.

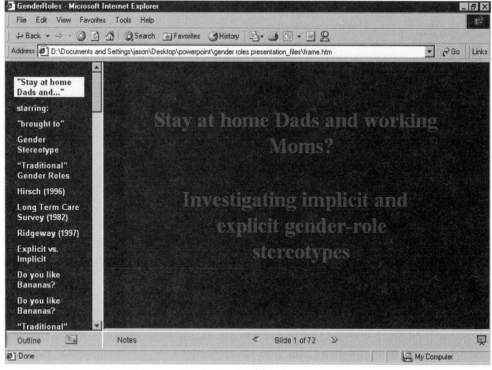

Figure 4-6   A PowerPoint presentation exported to a Web page.

A good Web site keeps a consistent look and feel, and usually you'll need to tweak imported Web pages in FrontPage to maintain this. In some cases, you'll need to heavily edit imported content to extract the desired sections and format the content in a way that meshes well with the rest of the page and the site. In these cases, it can often be easier to simply use FrontPage's import capabilities, if the file format you want to import is supported. Using FrontPage's import facilities prevents any extra formatting and HTML code from being inserted by the exporting application, making the content easier to work with in FrontPage.

Deciding whether to import content directly into FrontPage or to export content to a Web page using the program that created the content usually requires examining the applications involved and their capabilities. While there are no established rules about making this decision, here are some general recommendations.

If the application that created the content is capable of exporting Web pages, test out this export capability. Export the content to a Web page and then open the page in FrontPage and see how easy it is to integrate it with your other Web pages and content. ("Step 5: Create Your Web Site" gives you the full details on working with Web pages in FrontPage.) Especially when dealing with self-contained content such as PowerPoint presentations, this can work very well, often providing extra features and special formatting that would be difficult to do with FrontPage.

If you need to merge the content with other content within a single Web page, it may be simpler to import the file directly into FrontPage and then work with the data. If the content is already in a file format that FrontPage can import, there's nothing more to do. Otherwise, open the file in the program that created it and save the content into a supported file format (see Tables 4-1, 4-2, and 4-3 for supported file formats).

Images present their own set of issues. In general, all images used in a Web page should be either in the GIF or JPEG image formats. If you place a different type of image in a Web page, FrontPage automatically converts the image into either a GIF image (if the image format contains 256 colors or less) or a JPEG image (if the image format uses more than 256 colors, such as a photograph would). For most users and circumstances, FrontPage does a fine job of converting images, and you could use it to do all the image conversion work for your Web site.

However, if the quality or size of the image is important, or if you need to do something sophisticated like creating an image with transparency, you'll find it to your advantage to perform the conversion process using either the program that created the image or a stand-alone image editor, such as Adobe Photoshop, PaintShop Pro, or Microsoft PhotoDraw. If the program has a Save For Use On The Web function or similar command, consider using it. Commands like this usually walk you through saving the image as a GIF or JPEG file, choosing the proper amount of compression (balancing file size with image quality), or making part of the image transparent, saving you some guesswork. Figure 4-7 shows a screen from Microsoft PhotoDraw's Save For Use In Wizard.

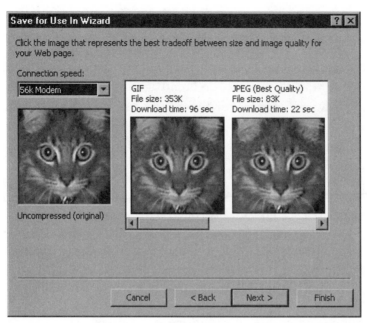

Figure 4-7   Converting an image to an appropriate format using an image editor's wizard.

TIP   *It's best to avoid using large images to prevent Web pages from taking too long to load. If you want to display a large, high-quality image, create a thumbnail (miniature version) of the image that is linked to the full-size image. This allows the Web page to load quickly, and if visitors want to see the high-resolution image, they can click the hyperlink to display the larger image. There is no hard rule about image sizes, but generally, if your page takes longer than 30 seconds to load over a 28.8 connection, you should make your images smaller or remove some of them. For more information about working with images in FrontPage, see "Step 5: Create Your Web Site."*

Creating New Digital Content

Not all content for your Web site is going to be available in digital format. Some of it will exist in print form and yet more will need to be created from scratch.

In general, the new content falls into two categories: images and documents. Images are usually created using a digital camera, a scanner, or from scratch using an art program of some sort. Documents are generally created from scratch using a word processor or spreadsheet program, although some companies will give in to the urge to scan printed documents that aren't already available in digital format.

Digital Images

Images are an important type of content for most Web sites. Acquiring and importing images into the computer thus is a fairly important task for most companies with a Web site.

There are several ways to create new digital images for use on a Web site. Photographs can be scanned into the computer using a scanner, imported using a PhotoCD picture disk or online image processing service, or they can be taken using a digital camera and directly imported into the computer. Digital images can also be created in the computer using an art program. The following sections help you get an overview of how digital image resolution works, get images into the computer no matter what method you choose, and also help your company decide which method will work best for future image acquisition.

Dots per Inch and Image Resolution

The whole subject of dots per inch (dpi) and image resolution can be confusing. Because it's a subject that you'll need to deal with any time you attempt to scan images into the computer, print them out, or modify their size and resolution, we provide a brief summary on image size, dpi, and image resolution.

Two factors determine the size and resolution of an image: dpi and resolution (pixels). All images on a computer monitor are displayed at 96dpi, so the only way to increase the quality onscreen is to increase the resolution.

However, when discussing photographs to scan or images to print, the situation gets a little contradictory. When scanning a photograph, size (resolution) can't be changed, so to get a higher quality image into or out of the computer, you need to increase the dpi. Similarly, when printing an image, if you keep the resolution (size) the same or lower it, but increase the dpi, you end up with a possibly smaller, but more richly detailed printout. (Although a 300dpi image and a 96dpi image will look the same on screen, the 300dpi image will look *much* better when printed out on a high-resolution printer.)

NOTE *Inkjet printers can print upwards of 1440dpi, but you don't need to create 1440dpi images to make the best use of these printers (and please don't—the resulting images would be gigabytes in size). A 300dpi image yields finely detailed printouts on a 1440dpi inkjet printer and increasing the dpi further doesn't provide a large increase in image quality.*

When you scan an image, the dpi you specify controls the resolution (size) of the image. For example, a four-by-six-inch photograph scanned at 150dpi makes a roughly 900x600-pixel image—just a bit bigger than full screen for a computer using the 800x600 screen resolution. You can then crop this image a bit and save it as an 800x600-sized image at 96dpi for use as a large image on the Internet.

Here are some recommendations for resolution, image size, and dpi:

- Scan images at whatever dpi necessary to get the size of image you want (150dpi yields a 900x600 image from a four-by-six-inch photo).

- Save images for use on the Internet or computer screens at 96dpi.

- Save images intended for high-quality printouts at between 150dpi and 300dpi, depending on the resolution of the printer and the importance of quality.

Digital Cameras

The best way to quickly and easily acquire images for use on a Web site is with a digital camera. Digital cameras are here to stay, and they are already replacing standard film cameras for many businesses and organizations—especially those that need to take lots of pictures for use on the Web (such as real estate professionals).

Digital cameras offer numerous advantages. They're the fastest way to get an image into the computer because there is no need to develop prints. Most have a small display screen so that you can instantly view captured photos—and immediately delete any that you don't like. The image quality on most new megapixel digital cameras (cameras that take images at 1024x768 resolution or higher) are more than adequate for any Web site work, and even print work can be accommodated by the highest resolution cameras (though not *quite* as well as standard film).

The biggest drawbacks with digital cameras are cost, battery life, and complexity. They're still pretty expensive, although this is changing, especially for midrange or low-end cameras (which are now usually sufficient for Web site work). A smaller downside to digital cameras is their typically voracious appetite for batteries. (Stock up on rechargeable batteries if your camera doesn't come with them.) Also, digital cameras are more complex to operate than normal film cameras and have a slightly larger learning curve than normal cameras.

TIP　*If you're in the market for a digital camera, we strongly urge you to consider getting one that has a USB interface, unless you have or plan to get a memory card reader (preferably USB) for your computer. The USB interface makes transferring images from the camera faster and much easier to configure, and it is now a standard feature on most cameras. Also, consider getting a camera with a zoom lens. Even a moderate two or three times magnification zoom provides a lot of flexibility when taking pictures.*

Here are some recommendations for using digital cameras for Web site image acquisition:

- Configure your camera to take pictures at the highest resolution you think your company may require. If you *know* that the images will never be used anywhere other than on the Internet or in a computer, it may be adequate to take pictures at 896x592 or similar resolution. You could even shoot images at 640x480 if the images will never be used full screen or for print work. If it's at all possible that the images will be used for high-quality printouts, take images at 1440x960 resolution or higher.

- Even if you don't require high-resolution images, configure your camera to use the highest or second-highest quality setting available. Some cameras offer an uncompressed image quality setting, which makes images much larger and generally should be avoided unless you are doing high-resolution print work.

- After taking pictures, consider transferring them into a separate subfolder located in your central content folder.

- Give images a short but descriptive name so that it's easy to tell what they are at a glance.

Scanning Photos

One of the most popular ways to get images into the computer is to take pictures using a standard camera, get prints made, and then scan the prints using a scanner.

Scanning photos has a low upfront cost associated with it: standard cameras are relatively inexpensive and of high quality, film isn't very expensive, and excellent flatbed scanners can be purchased for $100 or less. It's also the only way to get existing photos into the computer, and it's still the best way to get extremely high-quality images into the computer (although digital cameras generally suffice for all but the highest-quality requirements).

TIP *Flatbed scanners provide the most flexibility in the types of items that can be scanned, although sheet-fed scanners and photograph-specific scanners are usually less expensive. Also, if your company plans to scan photographs, a photograph scanner may prove easier to use than a flatbed scanner because there's no glass to smudge, and photographs won't slide around as much.*

However, if your company is frequently taking pictures for use on its Web site, scanning pictures isn't always the most effective way of getting pictures into the computer. Generally, a whole roll of film must be taken before prints can be made, and getting prints made takes both time and money. Once prints are made, scanning them can also take a fair amount of time and patience.

TIP *If you're in the market for a scanner, we recommend picking up a USB scanner that's supported by Windows 2000. USB scanners are easy to set up and fast, and even if your company doesn't have Windows 2000 yet, it's likely that in the future it will.*

Here are some recommendations for scanning images into the computer:

- Scan images the largest size you might need, and keep these high-resolution images in a separate high-resolution folder. For use on the Web, resize the images down to an appropriate size and save them in a different location or using a different filename.

- Scan images into the central content folder so that all people working on the Web site can find them easily.

- Give images a short but descriptive name so that it's easy to tell what they are at a glance.

Picture CDs and Disks

One way to get photographs into the computer if you don't have a digital camera or scanner is to pay an additional fee to get a picture CD, PhotoCD, or pictures on disk when getting regular print film developed.

This method eliminates the hassle of scanning pictures; however, it isn't very cost effective for most organizations. Generally, in addition to the cost of developing and creating prints, there is another charge of $3 to $20 per roll of film, depending on the scanning resolution and the company. It doesn't take too many rolls of film at this price before you've matched the price of a new scanner.

However, if there's a pressing need to acquire images and your company or organization doesn't have an alternative means to acquire images, paying to get pictures placed on CD or floppy disk at the time of developing can be an effective way to accomplish the task at hand.

Here are some recommendations to help you make the most of images from a CD or floppy disk:

- If you regularly use picture CDs or floppies, label the CDs or floppies well and store them somewhere that all people working on your Web site know about.

- The best way to take images from a picture CD or floppy is to browse to the images on the CD or floppy using Windows Explorer, and then copy the images directly into your central content folder, as shown in Figure 4-8. Alternatively, you can use the export function of the software included with the images to save the pictures as JPEG images, as shown in Figure 4-9.

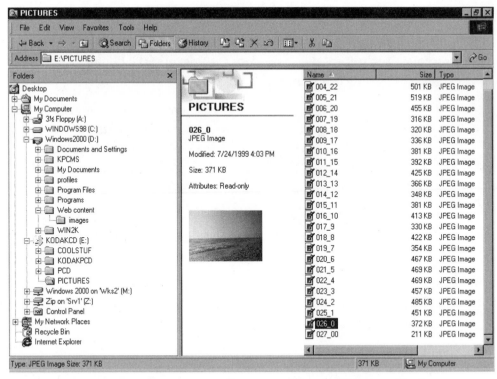

Figure 4-8   Manually taking images off a picture CD using Windows Explorer.

NOTE   *When you export images using the software included with the photos, you will usually lose some image quality and/or resolution. This usually isn't a problem, but if you're finicky about quality, take the original images off the CD using Windows Explorer and manually resize them to the proper size for your Web page using an image editor.*

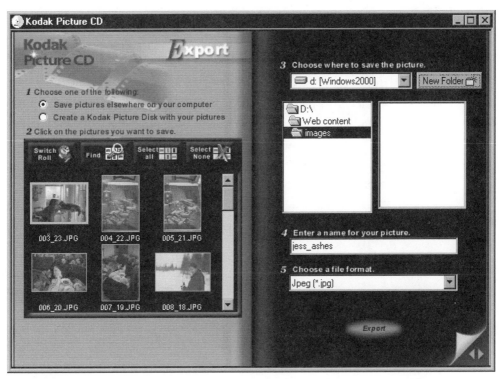

Figure 4-9   Exporting an image from a picture CD.

- Keep a close eye on the resolution and quality of the pictures exported. Typically the highest resolution available is around 1536x1024, which is far too big for use on the Web. However, it's usually preferable to take the high-resolution image and manually resize it to a more appropriate size for your Web site, instead of initially exporting a lower resolution image that might later turn out to be too small.

- Save images into the central content folder so that all people working on the Web site can easily find them.

- Give images a short but descriptive name so that it's easy to tell what they are at a glance.

Online Photo Services

Instead of paying to get your prints scanned and placed on a CD or floppy disk, many photo labs and services now offer to scan photos and place them on a secure Web site, from which you can then download them, as shown in Figure 4-10. This can provide somewhat quicker turnaround than picture CDs and disks, but in most respects it is otherwise identical—except that instead of taking pictures off a CD or disk they are downloaded over the Internet. Of course, if your company or organization needs high-resolution images and has a slow-speed Internet connection, this might not be the most effective means of acquiring images. Instead, use picture CDs, or preferably, get a scanner or digital camera.

Figure 4-10 A scanned roll of film at an online photo service.

Here are some recommendations for using an online photo service more effectively:

- Download the highest resolution version of the image you might need, since the higher resolution image may not be available later. In general, it's best to download a high-resolution image, make a copy of it, and then resize it for use on your Web site.

- Depending on the processing company, you may need to convert the images you download into JPEG (.jpg) images using their software before you can work with the images on your Web site.

- Make sure to download the images you want to use promptly. Some services keep images posted for only 30 days.

- Save images into the central content folder so that all people working on the Web site can easily find them.

- Give images a short but descriptive name so that it's easy to tell what they are at a glance.

Documents

Documents are the other half of the new content equation, and unfortunately, not every document that belongs on your Web site is going to already exist, or at least not in digital form.

Dealing with Print Documents

If your company or organization has content that would be desirable to place on its Web site, but you can't find a digital version of it, here's a suggested course of action:

1. **Look again.**

   We can't emphasize enough how much easier it is to use content that's already in digital form than it is to bring a print document into the computer.

2. **Retype the document.**

   Unless the document is really long, and even if it is, consider retyping any print documents that you want to use on your Web site. This is especially true for documents that have small typefaces, complex layouts or graphics, or are in poor condition. It's usually less hassle than scanning and performing Optical Character Recognition (OCR), and many documents won't need to be entirely retyped—just those sections that are needed for your Web site.

3. Scan the document and use an OCR program.

Although OCR programs have greatly improved and are now quite useful, unless you have a long document that needs to be placed in its entirety (or almost in its entirety) on your Web site, it's usually faster to retype a document than it is to scan it, run it through the OCR program, and then correct mistakes.

TIP   *OCR programs are stand-alone programs that convert a scanned document into text that can be used in a word processing program or Web page editor. They can provide an easy way to digitize existing, typewritten content, but do produce errors in the scanned documents. Therefore, we recommend that you carefully evaluate the amount of time involved in correcting scanned documents before relying heavily on OCR programs.*

4. Save the document to the central content folder.

After finding, retyping, or scanning the content, save it to your central content folder with a descriptive filename so that the file can be identified easily.

Creating New Documents

When creating new content for use on a Web site, you can take specific steps to make the content import into FrontPage more elegantly:

- Create any large amounts of text you want to use on your Web site using Microsoft Word or another word processing program, and then either save the document in Word format for importing into FrontPage or save it directly as an HTML document that FrontPage can then edit. While FrontPage is a passable text editor, it's much easier and more efficient to create content of any substantial length in a dedicated word processor.

- Avoid using complex formatting or graphics in documents. These generally don't import accurately into FrontPage and are best created later using FrontPage. An exception to this rule is when the program used to create the content has special HTML output capabilities that enable it to handle complex formatting or documents. However, these exported pages may prove difficult to edit in FrontPage, so test out this capability before you rely on it extensively.

- Before creating a large amount of content with a particular application, test out how well the content can be imported into FrontPage or exported to HTML from the application. Knowing the limitations of the process beforehand can save a lot of time and money in the long run.

- Save new documents in the central content folder with a useful filename that enables all people working on the Web site to easily identify the document.

Organizing Content and Planning Your Web Site

The organization and structure of a Web site rarely turns out well unless it is planned beforehand. Failing to plan and organize a Web site generally leads to a site that is confusing and ineffective at the job of presenting information to visitors.

Gathering all or most of your content together in one place is a good first step in planning your Web site's structure because it gives you an understanding of the content the Web site will contain. After doing this, we recommend that you sit down and organize the content, and then draw up a preliminary Web site plan.

NOTE   *The contrarian position to all this organizing and planning is that although it's true that Web sites created without much thought given to organization generally turn out to be confusing and ineffectual, it's OK to create one of these sites as a starting point if it suits your company or organization. Just keep in mind that at some point you'll probably want to restructure your site into a more effective form.*

Organizing Your Content

After you've rounded up the content for your Web site, many companies find that it makes a lot of sense to organize it before starting work on the site—both physically in the central content folder and logically for the structure of the Web site.

There are a number of different ways to organize content in your central content folder. One method that works well is to place content into folders depending on what action needs to be done with it. For example, a high_priority folder could store important content, or a possible_content folder could store content that you're not yet sure belongs on the Web site. Within these folders you could further organize the data by subject, source, and data type (i.e., documents and images).

In addition to deciding how to physically organize your content, you might want to work on some more abstract content organization. One way to do this is to sit down with a pad of paper and poke around the central content folder, making notes of what you have available and creating some logical groupings. The organization you decide upon may or may not be reflected in the folder structure of your central content folder.

It's more important to get an idea of how the content should be logically organized on your Web site than to actually organize it into separate folders.

We can't tell you exactly how to organize your content, since the content usually dictates this, but here are some recommendations to help with the process:

- Look closely at the Web site's purpose and the content that you identified as important in "Step 2: Develop a Content Strategy" and keep this focus central in your mind.

- Organize content logically and intuitively by subject. For example, a Web site designed to advertise or sell products would do well to organize content into product information, company information, and support information categories. This makes sense and is intuitive for visitors, since they match key topics that visitors will probably look for.

- Try not to organize your content in a way that leaves any categories with too much content or too little. If you find this happening, consider splitting or merging the categories, or creating subcategories.

Creating Your Site Plan

At this point you may want to actually sketch out the design for your Web site. Simple as it sounds, this is one of the more important parts of the Web-site-creation process, since the way in which you structure the Web site determines how easy and intuitive it is for visitors to use.

To create a plan for your Web site, sit down with a pad of paper or create a new Word document in Outline view. Pull out any notes you took on the content available for the Web site (see the section "Organizing Your Content" earlier in this step). Also take out the document you prepared in "Step 2: Develop a Content Strategy" that lists the purpose of the Web site and what it should accomplish, how the site will benefit your company or organization, what kind of content should be used, and the target audience for the Web site. This document gives the direction for your Web site, so we suggest that you review it thoroughly before creating your site plan.

When actually creating the site plan, most organizations will want to start with the home page—the Web page that is first displayed when visiting a Web site. The home page acts as the top of the outline that is your Web site. Briefly list what content should be contained here—perhaps a summary of the Web site, as well as short leaders on the site's most interesting or frequently accessed content. (For more help with this, see the section "Creating an Effective Home Page" in "Step 6: Polish Your Pages.") Then write down the categories for the next level of your Web site. Each of these categories will be a page on your Web site and a navigational link for your site if you make a navigation bar or set of hyperlinks for your site (you'll probably want to). As discussed in the section "Organizing Your Content" earlier in this step, the categories should be logical and intuitive to visitors. Also, the second-level headings (the first level below the home page) should provide users with an accurate summary of the content in your Web site.

TIP   *Allow room for additional pages and content when creating your site plan, especially when creating your second-level headings (those right under the home page). Redesigning a Web site to accommodate new content can be resource intensive as well as inconvenient to visitors who have learned your site layout or bookmarked individual pages in the Web site. If you anticipate adding content, leave room for it in the site plan.*

TIP   *You may find it useful to have a couple pages at the top level—the same level as the home page. These pages are typically pages designed to help users navigate your site, such as a Table of Contents page, a Search page, or maybe a Feedback page.*

While not absolutely necessary, we recommend taking at least a quick pass through the entire site, creating a diagram of what pages should be created and what content belongs on each page. Creating this Web site plan will not only make your Web site more coherent, intuitive, and effective but also make it easier to delegate Web site work.

TIP   *Try to avoid making too many levels in your Web site. From the home page, the most important content should be one click away, and all important content should ideally be no more than three clicks away for most sites. (Larger sites may need to have additional levels, but avoid it if possible.) Keeping information accessible with a low number of clicks makes accessing information faster and easier for visitors. It also increases the chance that visitors will stay rather than get impatient and leave the site.*

TIP *Besides watching out for a Web site structure that's too deep, you also need to avoid making the structure too wide (too many pages at the same level). This is especially true for the second level of pages (the first under the home page). Too many second-level pages will overload the site's navigation bars (which usually display all second-level pages) with too many options. Although there are no rules about how many links are too many, navigation bars (and Web pages in general) lose their effectiveness if there are too many options to choose from. There are exceptions and ways around this, but in general, limit your navigation bars to fewer than ten links, and possibly no more than five, depending on your page design.*

Summary

This step walked you through the last phase of Web site planning—collecting, creating, and organizing your company or organization's content—before you actually start creating pages. This step involves preparing a directory to store all content before it's actually added to the Web site, collecting existing digital content, creating new digital content, organizing the content, and then creating a plan for your Web site's structure. The actual process of creating and editing Web pages and constructing your Web site starts in "Step 5: Create Your Web Site."

CREATE YOUR WEB SITE

Featuring:

- Working with Web Sites in FrontPage
- Overview of the FrontPage Interface
- Managing Files in FrontPage
- Creating Basic Web Pages
- Managing Web Site Work

F rontPage 2000 is a powerful yet easy-to-use program that you can use to create, edit, and manage Web sites. FrontPage has a look and feel similar to Microsoft Word, so creating Web pages with FrontPage is much like creating documents in Word. If you are already a Word user, you will find FrontPage easy to learn and use.

This step introduces the FrontPage interface, helping you to create your FrontPage web. You also learn how to view your site, manage the files on your site, and create Web pages.

NOTE   *If there are capabilities that you require that aren't provided by FrontPage, you might need to use another program or hire an outside consultant. Keep in mind, though, that more sophisticated work can be done in another program or by an outside consultant and then easily integrated into your FrontPage Web site.*

NOTE *FrontPage 2000 contains a feature called Personalized Menus And Toolbars. To streamline the program's interface, this feature hides the menu commands and toolbar buttons that you use infrequently. To view the hidden menu commands, click the downward-pointing arrowheads at the bottom of the menu. Click the downward-pointing arrowheads on the far right side of a toolbar to display any hidden toolbar buttons. To turn off this feature, choose the Tools menu's Customize command, click the Options tab, and clear the Menus Show Recently Used Commands First check box and the Standard And Formatting Toolbars Share One Row check box.*

Working with Web Sites in FrontPage

The first thing you need to do when actually creating your Web site is to create or open your FrontPage web. A FrontPage *web*, as FrontPage calls it, is basically the local version of your Web site, which is stored in a folder somewhere on your company network. You perform all Web site work on the FrontPage web, and after testing it for errors, you publish the FrontPage web to your Web hosting company's Web server, which then makes the Web site accessible to everyone on the Internet.

TIP *Although you can avoid using FrontPage's Web site management capabilities and use FrontPage to create only pages, using FrontPage to manage your Web site saves a lot of time, while providing additional functionality and decreasing errors in your site, such as broken hyperlinks.*

The following sections show you how to create new FrontPage webs, as well as open and close existing FrontPage webs and Web pages.

Creating Web Sites

To begin creating the Web pages that make up your Web site, you first need to create a FrontPage web. To do this, FrontPage provides a number of Web site wizards or templates that you can use. If you choose a wizard, you then need to step through the wizard, answering the questions it asks and selecting options for your web.

TIP *The terms* web *and* Web site *are used interchangeably, although to be technical, a* web *is what FrontPage calls a series of grouped pages while they are inside FrontPage. After the web is published on a Web server, it is then called a* Web site.

Choosing a Web Site Template or Wizard

FrontPage provides several templates and wizards to help you create a web. To create a Web site using FrontPage, follow these steps:

1. Start FrontPage.

Click the Start button, choose the Programs menu, and then click Microsoft FrontPage.

2. Create a new web.

To do this, choose the File menu's New command, and then choose Web from the submenu.

3. Choose a template or wizard.

In the New dialog box, shown in Figure 5-1, select the template or wizard you want to use to create your Web site. Choosing a template creates a Web site with some predesigned pages that you can use as templates for your own content. Wizards take you through a series of dialog boxes that ask you questions, and then create typical pages for you using the information you provided. Click the One Page Web icon or click the Empty Web icon if you don't want or need to have pages created for you.

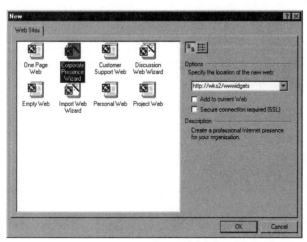

Figure 5-1   Creating a new web from a template or wizard.

TIP *You can create a new web out of pages you created previously, regardless of what program you used to create the Web pages. To do this, either choose the Import Web Wizard when choosing a template or wizard or, if you want to create a new web out of an entire folder, choose the File menu's Open Web command, find the folder that you want to convert to a web, and then click the Open button. When FrontPage asks whether you want to add FrontPage information to the folder, click Yes. Otherwise, your Web site won't have full FrontPage functionality. If you want to keep a copy of the site before editing it in FrontPage, make a copy of the Web site before converting it to a FrontPage web.*

4. Choose the location where your web should be stored.

Type the location where you want to store your web in the Specify The Location Of The New Web text box. This is different from the location of your central content folder, which is discussed in "Step 4: Collect and Organize Your Content," but you may want to place it on the same drive or network share for convenience.

TIP *You get the most bang for your buck if you store your FrontPage web on a local computer running a Web server program. Typically this will be a Windows 2000 computer running Internet Information Services (IIS), but Windows NT 4 computers can also work well for this task. If a local Web server is already configured, you may be able to simply enter the Web server's address in the Specify The Location Of The New Web box, followed by your web's name, for example, http://wks2/mycompany. See the Appendix "Set Up Your Web Site on a Local Web Server" for detailed help with getting your Web site created on a local Web server.*

5. Click OK, and proceed through the wizard, if chosen.

Click OK. If you chose a wizard, follow the instructions provided, as described in the next section.

Using FrontPage Web Wizards

Using FrontPage's Web wizards is an efficient way to rapidly create a Web site, and is especially useful for companies or organizations that don't have a clear idea of how their site should be structured. When you use a FrontPage wizard, FrontPage creates many of the essential pages for your web, based on the information you type into the various screens. Although these Web pages will need some modifications and you'll still need to insert your own content, they can streamline the process of creating your initial pages.

To use a wizard such as the Corporate Presence Web Wizard (as discussed here; other wizards are similar), choose a wizard and then follow these steps:

1. Launch the wizard.

Start FrontPage and choose a Web site wizard, as discussed in the previous section. In the first screen of the wizard, click Next.

TIP   *If you decide that you want to change something you previously entered, click the Back button.*

2. Select which pages to create using the wizard.

Select the check boxes corresponding to the Web pages you want in your web, and then click Next (see Figure 5-2).

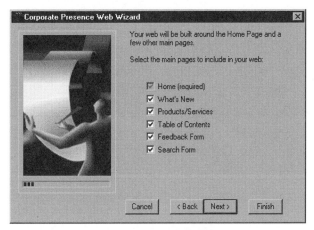

Figure 5-2   Selecting pages to include in your web.

3. Select the content to include on your home page.

Select the check boxes corresponding to the sections you would like on your home page (the first page of your Web site), and then click Next (see Figure 5-3).

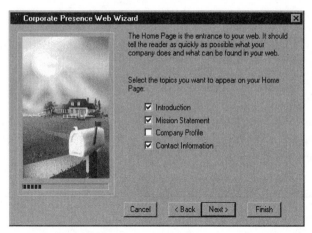

Figure 5-3　Specifying which sections to include on your home page.

4. Specify what content should be on other pages.

FrontPage asks what sections you'd like to include on each of the pages you chose to include in your web. Select the check boxes corresponding to the sections you would like (you can add more later), and click Next after each screen.

TIP　*If you chose to include a Feedback Form on your Web site, you'll be asked what fields to include and whether to use a Tab-Delimited Format for collected data. Choose the fields you think you want, and don't worry too much about the format question—it's easily changed later. See "Step 7: Add Interactivity to Your Web Site" for more information on creating and modifying Web page forms.*

5. Specify what content should be on other pages.

Select the check boxes for what items you would like at the top and bottom of every page, and then click Next (see Figure 5-4).

TIP　*What you put at the top and bottom of each page in your Web site is fairly important; however, it's also easily changed. So don't feel that you need to immediately decide how to lay out your navigation bars, headers, and footers. "Step 6: Polish Your Pages" helps you work out these issues.*

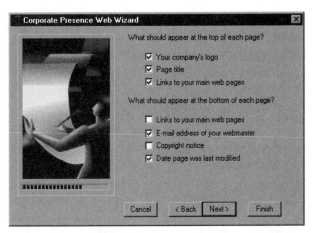

Figure 5-4   Specifying what to put in your headers and footers.

6. Choose whether or not to use Under Construction icons.

Specify whether or not to mark unfinished pages with the Under Construction icon, and then click Next.

TIP   *Some people find the Under Construction icon irritating. We recommend that you completely finish a page before posting it to the Web, but if you want to mark pages that are unfinished, consider creating your own icon or choosing an icon different from the usual construction icon.*

7. Enter your company information.

Enter your company's name and address, click Next, and then enter your company's telephone numbers and e-mail addresses and click Next again.

8. Choose a theme for your Web site.

Click the Choose Web Theme button and select a coordinated look for your Web site. Select a theme from the list at the left, and see how the sample page looks with the selected theme applied in the preview on the right. To make the colors used more vivid or buttons and lines stand out more, select the Vivid Colors or Active Graphics check boxes. To include a background picture, select the Background Picture check box. Click OK when you're finished (see Figure 5-5).

TIP   *As with every other decision you make when creating a Web site using a wizard, the theme you choose can easily be changed after the wizard is finished.*

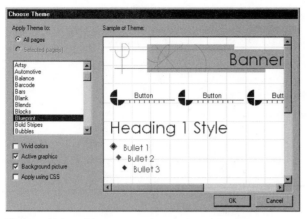

Figure 5-5   Choosing a theme for your web.

9. Finish the wizard.

Click Next, and then click Finish to create your web. If you want to immediately view the Web site tasks you need to accomplish (such as replacing sample content with original content), leave the Show Tasks View After Web Is Uploaded check box selected; otherwise, clear it.

Opening and Closing Web Sites and Pages

The next time you use FrontPage after creating your FrontPage web, and every time thereafter, you need to open your web or Web pages to work on them. You do this the same way you would open a file in any other Windows program.

To open a web, choose the File menu's Open Web command. When FrontPage displays the Open Web dialog box, select the folder containing the web from the Look In drop-down list box or by using the Places bar, as shown in Figure 5-6. When you find the web you want to open, select it and then click Open. If the web is stored on a local Web server, you'll probably be asked to provide a username and password to access the Web site. Enter your username and password in the dialog box provided and click OK.

Figure 5-6 The Open Web dialog box.

NOTE *The Places bar is the Microsoft Outlook-style bar on the left of Open and Save dialog boxes in Microsoft Office 2000 and Windows 2000. It has useful short-cuts to places where data is frequently located.*

TIP *You can quickly open the last four webs you worked on by choosing the File menu's Recent Webs command and then choosing a web from the list. To have FrontPage automatically open the last web you worked on when you launch FrontPage, choose the Tools menu's Options command and then select the Open Last Web Automatically When FrontPage Starts check box.*

To open a Web page, choose the File menu's Open command. When FrontPage displays the Open File dialog box, select the folder containing the Web page from the Look In drop-down list box or by using the Places bar. When you find the Web page you want to open, select it and then click Open.

TIP *If you have a web open, you can double-click any file in the Folder List to open the file in Page view.*

To close a web, choose the File menu's Close Web command or quit FrontPage. To close an individual page, click the Close button on the page's title bar or choose the File menu's Close command.

Overview of the FrontPage Interface

Before we cover creating and managing your Web site with FrontPage 2000 in more detail, it helps to be more comfortable with the FrontPage 2000 interface.

FrontPage 2000 consists of several areas (shown in Figure 5-7), some of which will be familiar and some of which may be new to you. At the top of the window is a familiar menu bar—where the File, Edit, and other menus are located. Immediately below this is one or more toolbars, where the most frequently accessed features and functions of FrontPage are located.

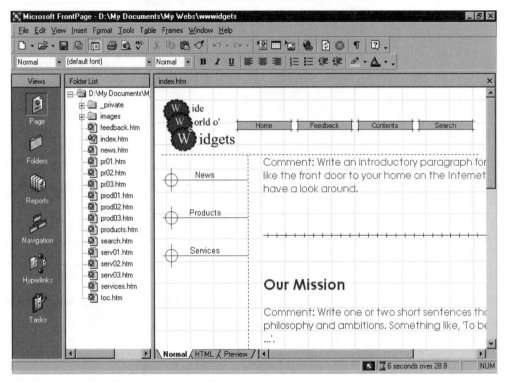

Figure 5-7 The FrontPage 2000 interface in Page view.

Below the menu bar and toolbars is the heart of the FrontPage 2000 interface—the tri-pane display. The three panes are the Views bar (similar to Outlook's Outlook bar), the Folder List (similar to Windows Explorer's Folder List), and the page or information pane, which typically displays a Web page for editing.

Using Views to View Your Web Site

The Views bar provides six different views that you can use to view and work with your Web site. Each view specializes in a different aspect of Web site creation and management. To open a particular view, click its icon on the Views bar. Each view is discussed in detail in the next sections.

Using the Page and Folders Views

You use the Page view for most of your work in FrontPage. With Page view you can edit pages as well as manipulate files in the Folder List.

Folders view is a more specialized view for working with files. It uses the pane in which you would normally edit a Web page and instead displays the contents of the currently selected folder.

To use Page view or Folders view, click the appropriate icon on the Views bar. To open a file in any view, double-click it. To move a file, drag it to the desired folder. FrontPage automatically updates any changed links when you move a file. To copy a file, drag the file to the folder you want while pressing the right mouse button, and then choose Copy Here from the shortcut menu (see Figure 5-8).

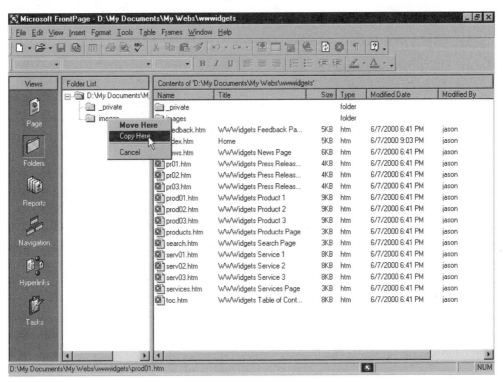

Figure 5-8 Copying a file in Folders view.

Using the Reports View

The Reports view is where you can quickly find out the vital statistics of your web: how much server space it takes, how many broken links you have, what tasks and pages are assigned to the various people working on your Web site, and whether any pages take too long to download.

To use the Reports view, click the Reports icon on the Views bar. To view a report, double-click its name (see Figure 5-9). To return to the Site Summary report after viewing a report, select Site Summary from the drop-down list box on the Reporting toolbar.

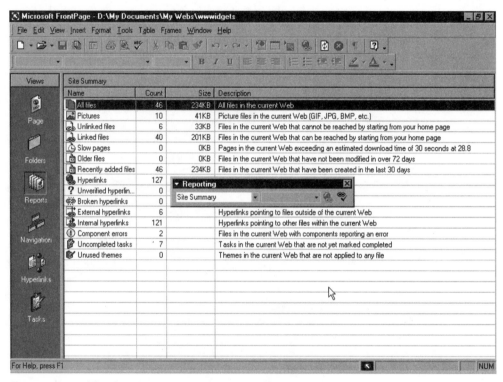

Figure 5-9   The Site Summary report in the Reports view.

NOTE   *The Reports view is also discussed in "Step 8: Deploy Your Web Site" because of its usefulness in monitoring and testing your Web site.*

Using the Navigation View

The Navigation view is where you control the structure of your web for the purposes of automatically created navigation bars; only pages that are in the Navigation view appear on navigation bars. (Navigation bars are discussed in "Step 6: Polish Your Pages.") If you keep it up to date (by adding new pages you create to it), the Navigation view is also a very efficient way to quickly open pages or get an overall feel for your Web site's layout.

To use the Navigation view, click the Navigation icon on the Views bar. Click a plus sign on a page icon to expand the page's hidden subtree, or click a minus sign to collapse a subtree. To add a page to the Navigation view, drag it from the Folder List to the appropriate location on the navigation tree. To delete a page from the Navigation view, right-click it and choose Delete from the shortcut menu.

TIP   *If you don't want a page to be included in navigation bars, instead of deleting it from the Navigation view, select the page and then click the Included In Navigation Bars button on the Navigation toolbar.*

Use the buttons on the Navigation toolbar, which usually floats above the Navigation view, to work with pages in the Navigation view, as shown in Figure 5-10. To resize the Navigation view, choose a scaling factor from the Zoom drop-down list box. To rotate the view, click the Portrait/Landscape toolbar button. To change whether a page should appear on navigation bars, toggle the Included In Navigation Bars toolbar button. To hide all pages other than those beneath the currently selected page, click the View Subtree Only toolbar button.

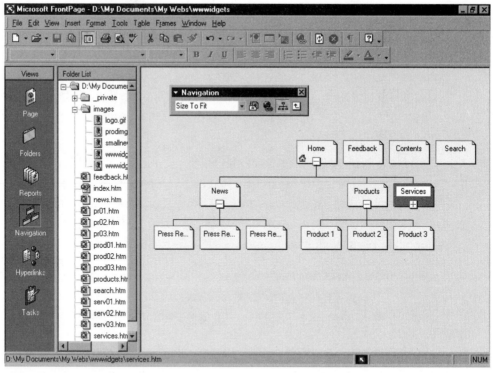

Figure 5-10 The Navigation view controls which pages appear on navigation bars.

Using the Hyperlinks View

You can use the Hyperlinks view to graphically display all the hyperlinks in a page, as well as all the pages that link to the selected page.

To use the Hyperlinks view, click the Hyperlinks icon on the Views bar. Select a page from the Folder List to view all hyperlinks to and from that page. To move around in the Hyperlinks view, click the background and drag your mouse to move the whole hyperlink structure. To expand the hyperlinks for a certain page, click the page's plus sign (see Figure 5-11). Broken hyperlinks show up as a line with a break in it.

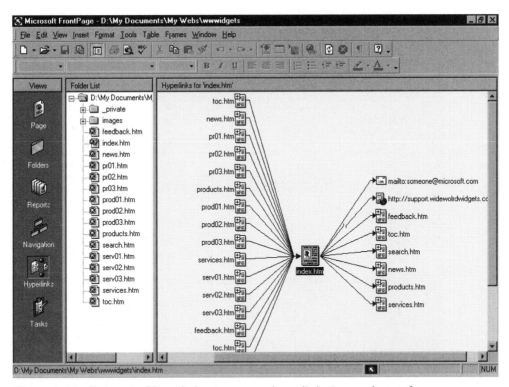

Figure 5-11 Using the Hyperlinks view to see hyperlinks into and out of your pages.

TIP   *To center the view on a certain page, right-click the page and choose the short-cut menu's Move To Center command.*

Using the Tasks View

The Tasks view is useful for keeping track of Web site tasks that must be completed. It's a view that you'll probably want to become familiar with, especially if you need to coordinate Web site work with many people (covered in greater detail in the "Managing Web Site Work" section later in this step). You can use the Tasks view to create tasks for the pages you need to create or edit, search engines to submit to, or any other task related to your Web site.

To use the Tasks view, click the Tasks icon on the Views bar (see Figure 5-12).

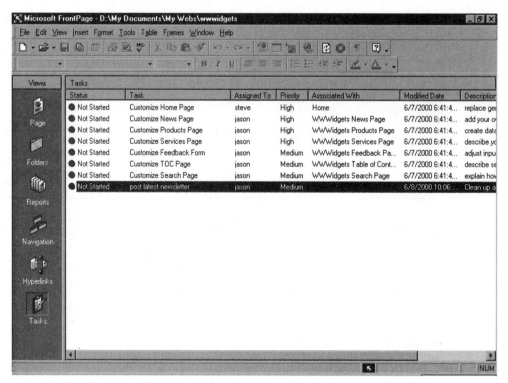

Figure 5-12   Using the Tasks view to maintain a list of web tasks that need to be done.

To add a new task, right-click in the Tasks view and choose New Task from the shortcut menu. Enter a task in the Task Name text box. Select a priority for the task using the Priority option buttons. Type a description for the task in the Description text box. Click OK when you're finished.

TIP   *To link a Web page to a new task, in the Folders or Page view, drag the desired page to the Tasks icon on the Views bar. When the Tasks view opens, drag the page into the view to create a new task with your page linked to it. You can then right-click the task later and choose Start Task from the shortcut menu to open the page and begin working on it.*

To edit a task, double-click a task to open it in its own window. Once the task is open, you can edit the task name, to whom the task is assigned, its priority, and description. Click OK when you're finished.

To mark a task as complete, right-click the task and choose Mark Task As Completed from the shortcut menu. To delete a task, right-click it and choose Delete from the shortcut menu. When FrontPage asks whether you're sure you want to delete the task, click OK.

TIP   *If you want to see tasks that you completed in the past, right-click in the Tasks view and choose Show Task History from the shortcut menu.*

Viewing Your Web Pages

When you're editing in Page view, FrontPage displays three different tabs at the bottom of the Web page: the Normal tab, the HTML tab, and the Preview tab. Each tab shows a different representation of the currently open Web page, and each has a different use:

- Use the Normal tab to create or edit your Web page visually, as if in a word processor.
- Use the HTML tab to work with color-coded, true HTML code.
- Use the Preview tab to view how your Web site would look in a browser.

Using these tabs to view your Web pages is discussed in the next several sections.

Using the Normal Tab

Use the Normal tab to do all of your Web page creating and editing. Enter text and add pictures and tables just like you would using Microsoft Word (see Figure 5-13). Because of how easy and powerful it is to edit Web pages using the Normal tab, throughout this book we assume that you're using the Normal tab to edit your Web pages (although some tasks also work using the HTML tab).

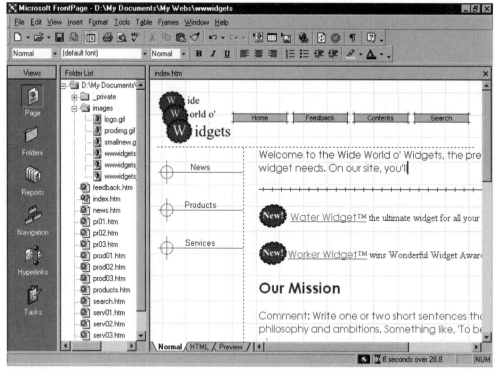

Figure 5-13   Editing a page using the Normal tab.

Using the HTML Tab

The HTML tab shows you a fully accurate, color-coded view of the HTML source code for your open Web page (see Figure 5-14). FrontPage 2000 preserves all changes you make to the source code and automatically updates your Normal and Preview tab's views when you switch to them. You can edit the source code like you would with a normal text editor, but you can also use FrontPage's tools to quickly add objects that would be time-consuming to code, such as tables. Simply use the tools as you would in the Normal tab, and FrontPage inserts the code into your page.

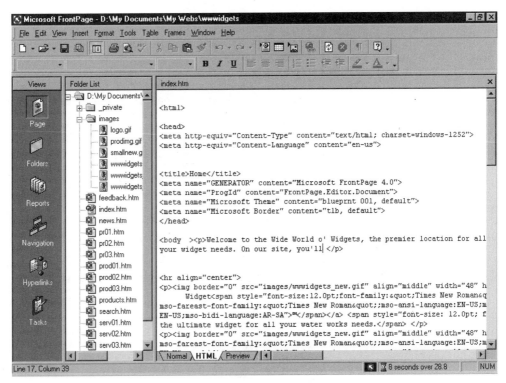

Figure 5-14   Working directly with code using the HTML tab.

TIP   *To customize how FrontPage formats your code, choose the Tools menu's Page Options command, click the HTML Source tab, and then specify how you want to format your code.*

Using the Preview Tab

The Preview tab shows your Web page displayed with Microsoft Internet Explorer's browser directly inside FrontPage. This permits you to quickly see how your page will appear before actually publishing it to a Web server. Click the hyperlinks just as you would in a normal Web browser to view other pages linked to from the current page. To go backward or forward to a page you previously viewed, right-click anywhere in the Preview tab and choose Back or Forward from the shortcut menu.

TIP Even though the Preview tab uses Microsoft Internet Explorer's browser for its display, we nonetheless recommend that you preview your page in both Internet Explorer and Netscape Navigator at several screen resolutions before publishing. This testing will eliminate many of the most glaring web design problems and compatibility errors. For more information on testing, see "Step 8: Deploy Your Web Site."

NOTE   For more information on making a page compatible with other browsers, see the "Creating an Effective Home Page" section in "Step 6: Polish Your Pages."

TIP   To preview a page in your default browser, click the Preview In Browser toolbar button. To view the page in a different browser, preview the page in your default browser and then copy the address of the file from the browser's Address or Location text box to the Address or Location text box of your other browser.

Managing Files in FrontPage

After creating or opening your FrontPage web, you'll most likely need to perform some file management tasks, such as adding new pages or folders (and importing files), moving and copying files, renaming files, and deleting files and folders. The following sections explain how to carry out these tasks, which you'll find yourself performing frequently throughout the life of your Web site.

As mentioned earlier, FrontPage is quite a capable site management tool in addition to being a top-of-the-line Web page editor. In fact, you'll probably want to perform all file management chores directly in FrontPage, instead of using Windows Explorer. Besides being easier, using FrontPage to manage the files in your Web site ensures that hyperlinks won't be broken by moving or renaming files. When you move or rename a file (which could be a Web page, image, or downloadable file) in your Web site using Windows Explorer, any hyperlinks to that file break, preventing visitors to your Web site from accessing the file. However, if you move or rename a file using FrontPage, all hyperlinks to that file are *automatically* updated.

Adding New Pages and Folders

To add a new Web page or folder to your web, right-click the folder in the Folder List to which you would like to add a page or folder, and then choose New Page or New Folder from the shortcut menu.

To import files, folders, or pages into your web, choose the File menu's Import command and then click the Add File, Add Folder, or From Web buttons to add pages to the import file list. After you've selected pages to import, click OK. Alternatively, open Windows Explorer, select the files you want to import, and drag them into the appropriate folder in the FrontPage Folder List (make sure you can view both Windows Explorer and FrontPage at the same time).

Moving and Copying Files

There are times when you'll need to move or copy files into different folders in your web, perhaps to keep all pages or files dealing with a certain part of your web in one spot. For example, if your company or organization publishes an online newsletter, you may want to create a separate directory in your web for all the newsletters. Similarly, you'll probably want to place all images on your Web site in the Images folder.

To move a file to another folder, click the file in Folder view or in the Folder List of Page view, and drag it to the desired folder in the Folder List.

To copy a file, drag the file to the desired folder by pressing the right mouse button instead of the left mouse button. When you release the button, choose Copy from the shortcut menu.

Renaming Files

To rename a file, right-click a file in the Folder List, and choose Rename from the shortcut menu. Type in a new filename or edit the existing one.

WARNING *Don't change the file's three-letter extension, or you won't be able to properly view or use the file.*

Deleting Files, Folders, and Webs

Even though it usually makes sense to leave most files on your Web site indefinitely, there are times when you might need to delete some. You might want to do this if you want to replace a file with a revised version, or if you need more space on your Web site.

Deleting items is quite easy. Simply right-click the file or folder you want to delete, and choose Delete from the shortcut menu. Or select the file or folder, and press the Delete key on your keyboard.

To delete an entire FrontPage web, right-click the highest-level directory in your web and choose Delete from the shortcut menu. FrontPage then displays the dialog box shown in Figure 5-15.

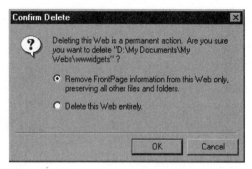

Figure 5-15 Deleting a FrontPage web.

If you want to keep the pages in your web but want to remove all FrontPage information from it, click the first option button and then click OK. (This is the best way to prepare a Web site for publication on a CD-ROM.) To delete everything in the web, click the Delete This Web Entirely option button and then click OK.

WARNING   *Files that are deleted in FrontPage do **not** go to the Recycle Bin. After you respond to FrontPage's confirmation, the files you deleted are immediately and permanently gone, so be careful.*

Creating Basic Web Pages

Creating new pages in FrontPage is just like creating new documents in any other Microsoft Office program. You can create a blank page or choose from a variety of templates and wizards.

To create a new page, choose the File menu's New command, and then choose Page from the submenu. Choose the template or wizard that best approximates the Web page you want to create, and then click OK, as shown in Figure 5-16.

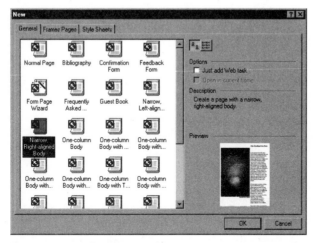

Figure 5-16 Creating a new page.

After creating a new page, it appears open in FrontPage ready for you to add your own content or modify the sample content if you chose a Web page template.

Saving and Exporting Web Pages

After you've created your Web page in FrontPage, you need to save it. Even though you probably haven't added anything to the page yet, this step is so important that it warrants coming first.

To save your Web page, either click the Save toolbar button or choose the File menu's Save As command. Choose the folder you want to use, and enter the name of your file in the File Name text box. Click the Change button, and enter a better title for the Web page in the Set Page Title dialog box. Click OK, enter the filename you want to use for the Web page in the File Name box, and click the Save button when you're finished, as shown in Figure 5-17.

Figure 5-17   Using the Save As dialog box to save or export your Web pages.

If the Web page contains new embedded files, such as an image that wasn't present in your Web site previously, the Save Embedded Files dialog box appears, as shown in Figure 5-18. Verify that you want to save all the files shown, that they are named appropriately, and in the proper folder. To change the name of the file, select it and click Rename. To change the folder in which the file will be saved, click the Change Folder button. To specify whether or not the file should be saved into your web at all, click the Set Action button. Click OK when you're finished.

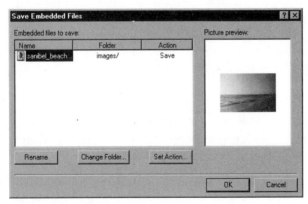

Figure 5-18 The Save Embedded Files dialog box.

TIP *Even though FrontPage will let you create a Web page with spaces or upper-case letters in its filename, don't use them. Filenames with spaces or uppercase letters may never cause problems if you stick with a Web hosting company that uses Windows 2000 or Windows NT Web servers, but if you move to a Unix-based Web server at some point, you could end up in big trouble. Unix deals with spaces and capitalization much differently than does Windows, and this could cause your entire Web site to break.*

TIP *To export your page, simply save the page to a folder that isn't a part of your FrontPage web. FrontPage will automatically bundle any included images with the page.*

Importing Text

Despite the multimedia emphasis of the Web, text is still the heart of most good Web pages. Besides being a clear and concise means of communicating to your visitors, text also downloads very quickly, can be indexed by search engines, and is usually easier to create than more visual forms of content. If you already have text in your central content folder ready to be inserted into a Web page, use the following procedure to insert the text into your Web page.

NOTE *The central content folder is the folder in which we recommend that you store all your content before bringing it into your FrontPage web, as discussed in "Step 4: Collect and Organize Your Content."*

1. **Position the cursor where you want to insert the text.**

   FrontPage will insert the entire contents of the file you specify at the current location of the cursor, so place the cursor somewhere suitable.

2. **Choose the Insert menu's File command.**

   FrontPage displays the Select File dialog box, as shown in Figure 5-19, which you use to find the file from which you want to import text.

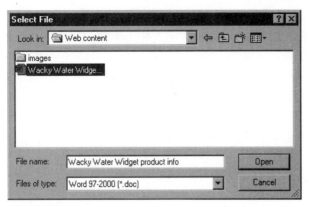

Figure 5-19 Inserting text into a Web page using the Select File dialog box.

3. Locate your central content folder.

Select the drive where your central content folder is located from the Look In drop-down list box. Navigate to your central content folder by double-clicking folders to open them. When you find it, double-click it to view the contents of the folder. (If the file is located elsewhere, open the appropriate folder.)

4. Choose the file type you're looking for.

Select the type of file you want to import from the Files of Type drop-down list box, or select All Files from this box if you're unsure.

5. Select the file you want to import, and click Open.

FrontPage converts the document into HTML code and imports the text into your Web page. The text you import appears as normal text in FrontPage, although you can view the HTML code using the HTML tab if desired.

Entering and Formatting Text

Enter text exactly as you would in a normal word processor. Click in the location where you want to add text, and enter the text. FrontPage, like Microsoft Word, underlines misspelled words as you type. Right-click them to see suggested spellings. You can also use the Spelling toolbar button to run a traditional spelling-check. The rest of the typical text-formatting tools are also here, and quite easy to use.

- To change the style of the text, for example, to make the text into a heading, select the text and choose the style you want from the Style drop-down list box on the toolbar.

TIP   *Using styles is a very effective way to standardize the look of pages across your Web site. For example, use the Normal style for most text, use Heading 1 for the page or Web site title, and Heading 2, 3, etc. for subsequent headings. If you want to modify the style itself, either apply a theme (discussed in "Step 6: Polish Your Pages") or consider using a style sheet.*

- To change the font, select the text and choose the font you want from the Font drop-down list box.

TIP   *Be careful which fonts you choose. If your visitors don't have the font you picked, another—perhaps drastically different—font will be substituted.*

- To change the font size, select the text and then choose the font size from the Font Size drop-down list box.

- Use the Bold, Italic, and Underline toolbar buttons to bold, italicize, or underline the selected text.

- Use the Align Left, Center, and Align Right toolbar buttons to change the alignment of the selected paragraph.

- Use the Numbering and Bullets toolbar buttons to make numbered or bulleted lists.

- To increase or decrease the indentation of a paragraph, image, or object, click the Increase Indent or Decrease Indent toolbar buttons.

- To highlight text with a particular color, or simply change the color of the selected text, click the down arrow next to the Highlight Color or Font Color toolbar buttons, and choose a color from the pop-up menu.

TIP   *Press the Enter key only at the end of a paragraph. If you press Enter at the end of every line, your Web page will look strange when displayed on a different-size monitor or in a different-size window.*

Creating Hyperlinks

A hyperlink is a piece of text or an image that when clicked takes the visitor to another page, image, or file. Hyperlinks are one of the most useful features of Web pages. They allow visitors to easily access information they're seeking and also provide a way for visitors to access related information they may not have otherwise sought out.

Although hyperlinks are indispensable tools, they are not without hazard. Hyperlinks leading to other Web sites can quickly lead visitors away from your site, something that you need to be careful about. In general, placing a hyperlink in a document is an invitation for visitors to follow the link, so only place links when you want to lead visitors elsewhere.

TIP   *If you want to include references to related information but don't want to explicitly send visitors away from the current page, make a related information column or section of the page with links to other pages and sites with more information.*

To create a hyperlink, select the text or image, and click the Hyperlink toolbar button. In the Create Hyperlink dialog box, select the file to which you want to link, or type the file's address in the URL text box. To make a hyperlink to an e-mail address, click the envelope icon in the Edit Hyperlink dialog box, shown in Figure 5-20, and then enter the e-mail address in the dialog box that's displayed.

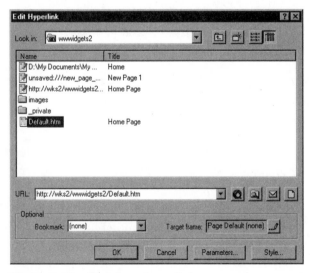

Figure 5-20   Creating a hyperlink.

To create a hyperlink within a Web page, called a bookmark, place the cursor where you want to allow visitors to be able to quickly link to (such as heading midway down a long page), and choose the Insert menu's Bookmark command. In the Bookmark dialog box, enter a short name for the bookmark in the Bookmark Name text box, and then click OK. To create a hyperlink to this bookmark, highlight the text you want to make into a link (most likely at the top of the page) and click the Hyperlink toolbar button. In the Create Hyperlink dialog box, select *the same page*, select the bookmark you created from the Bookmark drop-down list box at the bottom of the window, and click OK.

TIP   *Creating effective hyperlinks can be an art unto itself, but in general, all you need to do is make the linking text short and descriptive. No need to include the words* click here—*this is implicit. For example, use* <u>widgets</u> *instead of* <u>click here for widgets</u>.

Working with Images

Along with the standard image capabilities available in other Microsoft Office applications, FrontPage has a few special abilities that help make your use of images in Web pages more effective. The following sections explain how to insert images, modify image properties (including size and spacing), set alternative representations, and create thumbnail images.

Inserting Images

The easiest way to insert an image into a Web page is to find the image in the Folder List, and then drag it to the desired spot in your Web page. You can also use Windows Explorer to drag images directly from your central content folder into a Web page. FrontPage then converts the image into a JPEG or GIF file if the image is in another format.

Alternatively, click the Insert Picture From File toolbar button and select your image from the Picture dialog box, or click the Clip Art button in the Picture dialog box to insert a piece of clip art into your Web page.

To insert a horizontal line—a visual divider used to separate content elements—position the cursor where you want to place the horizontal line and then choose the Insert menu's Horizontal Line command. To modify the horizontal line's properties, double-click it.

Resizing Images

Some images just aren't the right size for your Web page. You can resize images by using either FrontPage or a stand-alone image editor. For most uses, FrontPage generally does a fine job.

NOTE   *You might want to use a stand-alone image editor such as Microsoft PhotoDraw instead of FrontPage's built-in tools to resize images with transparency (usually GIFs) or JPEG images that you notice degrade in quality when resized and resampled by FrontPage.*

TIP   *Keep in mind that you can only discard image information, not gain it; so avoid increasing the size of images by much. An image that is enlarged too much looks pixilated and ugly, something that doesn't reflect well on a Web site.*

The easiest way to resize an image in FrontPage is to click it to select the image, move the mouse over one of the sizing handles until the cursor turns into a dual-sided arrow, and then drag the outline of the image in or out to make the image smaller or bigger, as shown in Figure 5-21.

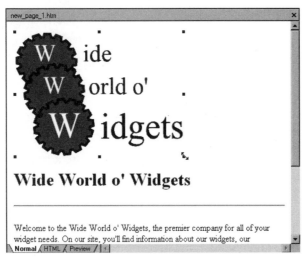

Figure 5-21 Resizing an image.

To precisely resize an image, right-click the image, choose Picture Properties from the shortcut menu, and then click the Appearance tab. Select the Specify Size check box and then adjust the width and height in pixels to the new size. Clear the Keep Aspect Ratio check box if it's okay to distort the image by adjusting the height and width non-proportionally.

NOTE   *In general, images shouldn't be sized by percent because they'll end up strangely distorted, the wrong size, or pixilated. Some exceptions are images used as horizontal lines and images used as visual dividers.*

If you reduce the size of an image, it's important to resample the image in order to reduce the file size. Otherwise, Web browsers still download the larger-sized image and simply display it sized smaller.

To resample an image, select the image after resizing it, and then click the Resample button on the Image toolbar, at the bottom of the FrontPage window. Alternatively, resize the image using a stand-alone image editor, which will automatically resample the image when you resize it.

Adjusting Image Layout

To adjust how text is laid out with an image—for example, how it's aligned with the image and how much spacing is in between the image and the text—right-click the image, choose Picture Properties from the shortcut menu, and then click the Appearance tab, as shown in Figure 5-22.

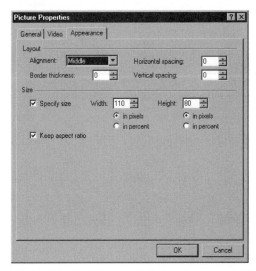

Figure 5-22 Changing the layout options for an image.

To specify how you want to align text adjacent to your image, choose an option from the Alignment drop-down list box. To add a border, specify a border width in the Border Thickness box. Use the Horizontal Spacing and Vertical Spacing boxes to adjust how much space to leave between the image and adjacent text or images.

TIP   *The best way to get a feel for what the Alignment options do is to type some text next to your image and then try out the different settings.*

Setting Alternative Image Representations

One way you can make a Web page more effective is to provide alternative text-based descriptions of your images. These descriptions are displayed while the images are loading (which on slow Internet connections can often take a while), or in browsers that have images disabled, and can help make your Web site usable for a wider audience.

TIP   *Setting alternatives is a good practice in general, but it is no substitute for creating pages that load quickly. In general, your Web pages should load in less than 30 seconds over a 28.8 connection. (See the Estimated Time To Download display on the lower right part of FrontPage's status bar for an estimate of how long the current page will take to load.) See "Step 6: Polish Your Pages" for more help on optimizing your Web pages.*

To specify what your alternative text should be, or to specify a low-resolution alternative image, right-click the image, choose Picture Properties from the shortcut menu, and then click the General tab, as shown in Figure 5-23.

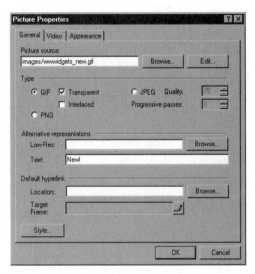

Figure 5-23 Setting alternative representations for an image.

Enter the text you want visitors to see when they cannot see your image in the Text box. To specify a low-resolution image to display while the full-size image is loading, click the Browse button next to the Low-Res text box, select the image you want displayed, and then click OK.

TIP   *In general, don't worry about providing a low-resolution version of an image unless you have a very large image on a Web page. If this is the case, consider making a thumbnail image for it instead.*

Creating a Thumbnail Image

You can use FrontPage's Auto Thumbnail tool to create a thumbnail image, or a small version of an image that is hyperlinked to the full-size version. When you use thumbnail images, visitors can quickly load and read your pages. If they want to view a specific full-size image, they can click that one image and wait for it to load—without waiting for a whole page of full-size images.

To create a thumbnail out of an image, click the image and then click the Auto Thumbnail toolbar button on the Picture toolbar.

TIP   *To change the way FrontPage creates Auto Thumbnails, choose the Tools menu's Page Options command and then click the Auto Thumbnail tab. Change the width of the thumbnail image, the border thickness, or bevel the edges of the image, and then click OK.*

TIP   *FrontPage's Auto Thumbnail feature is exceedingly handy but rather basic. To create fancier thumbnail image effects, use a stand-alone image editor such as Microsoft PhotoDraw or Adobe PhotoShop.*

Managing Web Site Work

If more than one person will be working on your company or organization's Web site, management of the efforts of all people involved becomes a critical issue. Allowing two or more people to work simultaneously on a Web site without taking a few pre-emptive measures is a reliable recipe for disaster. Fortunately, FrontPage 2000 provides some very effective tools that you can use to manage the work on your Web site and to avert the most common kinds of catastrophes.

The following sections show you how to configure FrontPage for use with multiple users and then how to manage the workflow.

Configuring Your Web Site for Multiple Users

In order to work with multiple users, several features require advance setup in FrontPage, such as work categories, usernames, review statuses, the ability to check out pages to a particular user for editing, and Web site security.

Setting Up Categories

FrontPage 2000 allows you to assign categories to files in your Web site. This helps you easily view the files for a particular category. For example, you might create a Products category for all files related to your products, or use the In Process category for pages that are still being constructed.

FrontPage comes preconfigured with 12 categories, but you may want to add or remove categories from this list to suit your company or organization's individual needs. To do so, follow these steps:

1. Right-click a file, and choose Properties from the shortcut menu.

This displays the Properties dialog box for the selected file. Note that it doesn't matter which file you click.

2. Click the Workgroup tab.

The Workgroup tab of the file's Properties dialog box (shown in Figure 5-24) is where you can assign a category, user, or review status to a file, or set up these lists.

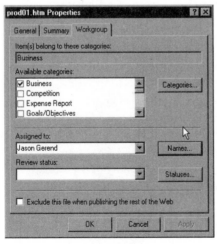

Figure 5-24 The Workgroup tab of a file's Properties dialog box.

3. Click the Categories button.

This displays the Master Category List dialog box, shown in Figure 5-25.

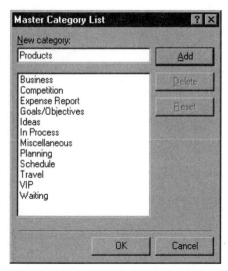

Figure 5-25 The Master Category List dialog box.

4. Add or delete categories.

To create a new category, enter the name of the category in the New Category box. To delete an existing category, select the category from the list and click Delete.

TIP   *You can always get the preset categories back by pressing the Reset button. However, doing this also deletes any categories you've created.*

Setting Up Usernames

FrontPage allows you to assign tasks and Web pages to individual users, but in order to do this, you need to create a list of usernames. To do so, follow these steps:

1. Right-click a file, and choose Properties from the shortcut menu.

This displays the Properties dialog box for the selected file. Note that it doesn't matter which file you click.

2. Click the Workgroup tab, and then click the Names button.

This displays the Usernames Master List dialog box, shown in Figure 5-26.

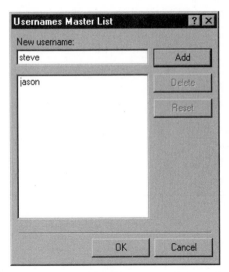

Figure 5-26 The Usernames Master List dialog box.

NOTE   *The usernames you set up here are used only for assigning tasks and pages in FrontPage. They do **not** affect permissions or security in any way. Those features need to be configured separately, and they are discussed later in this section.*

3.Add or delete users.

To create a new user, enter the user's login name in the New Username box. To delete an existing user, select the user from the list and click Delete.

TIP   *It's best to create usernames that match those used by your users to log on. When a user creates a task or checks out a document, FrontPage automatically records this information to the username used to log on to the FrontPage web. If the username you create in the Usernames Master List matches the user's logon name, everything will match up perfectly, eliminating potential confusion when assigning and completing tasks.*

Setting Up Review Statuses

Review statuses are a useful way of identifying the stage of the publishing phase for a particular file. For example, you could assign the Legal Review phase to a file to indicate that the file needs to be reviewed by the legal department of your company before being published to your Web site.

FrontPage comes preconfigured with four review statuses, but you might want to modify these to suit the way your company or organization works. The following steps help you accomplish this task:

1. **Right-click a file, and choose Properties from the shortcut menu.**

   This displays the Properties dialog box for the selected file. Note that it doesn't matter which file you click.

2. **Click the Workgroup tab, and then click the Statuses button.**

   This displays the Review Status Master List dialog box, shown in Figure 5-27.

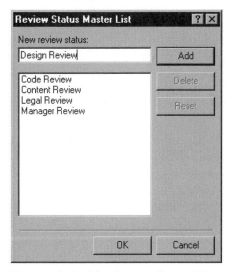

Figure 5-27 The Review Status Master List dialog box.

3. **Add or delete review statuses.**

   To create a new review status, enter the name of the review status in the New Review Status box. To delete an existing review status, select the status from the list and click Delete.

Enabling Document Check-In and Check-Out Capabilities

FrontPage 2000 comes with the ability to check out individual files to a particular user, during which time the file is unavailable for editing by other users. If you don't use this feature and have multiple users editing the Web site, you're almost certainly going to lose data when two users try to edit the same file at the same time.

In order to use document check-in and check-out capabilities, you need to enable it on your FrontPage web. To do this, follow these steps:

1. Choose the Tools menu's Web Settings command.

This displays the Web Settings dialog box, shown in Figure 5-28.

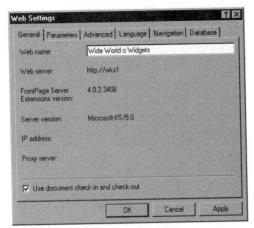

Figure 5-28   The Web Settings dialog box.

2. Select the Use Document Check-In And Check-Out check box.

This turns the feature on for the currently open FrontPage web. Click OK. FrontPage notifies you that it will take a couple of minutes to process this change, and asks whether you want to continue. Click Yes.

NOTE   *FrontPage may ask you to log on with a user account with sufficient privileges. If this happens, enter the username and password of a user with author permissions on this web.*

Setting Permissions on Your FrontPage Web

If your FrontPage web is stored on a local Web server, you can control which groups and users have the ability to browse, author, and administer the FrontPage web. This is the simplest way of preventing unauthorized employees from making changes to your Web site. However, FrontPage's security is only as good as that provided by your local Web server and network, so you may want to investigate the security of your network in general if security is of primary importance to your company or organization.

TIP   *If you need to implement separate permissions for part of your Web site, create a new FrontPage web for this part of your site and place the web within your main site. This adds a little hassle, since FrontPage treats subwebs as separate webs; however, once published to the Internet, they appear to be part of the same Web site to visitors.*

To configure the security settings for your FrontPage web, follow these steps:

1. Choose the Tools menu's Security command, and then choose Permissions.

This displays the Permissions dialog box, shown in Figure 5-29.

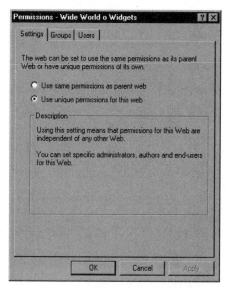

Figure 5-29   The Permissions dialog box.

2. Decide whether to use the parent web's permissions.

The default setting is to inherit the permissions of the root web on your local Web server. If you want to use different permissions for the currently open web, click the Use Unique Permissions For This Web option button.

TIP   *The root web on a local Web server is usually either left unused or used as an intranet Web site, for sharing information locally on your network. To see the permissions for it, open the web as you would your normal web, except instead of specifying a subdirectory (such as* http://websrv1/mycompany*), just enter the address of the Web server, for example,* http://websrv1*. Once open, choose the Tools menu's Security command, and then choose Properties.*

3. View the group permissions.

Click the Groups tab to view which user groups have permissions to the FrontPage web, as shown in Figure 5-30.

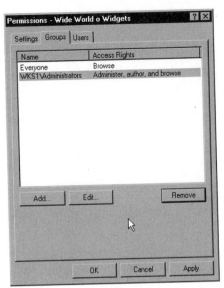

Figure 5-30 The Groups tab of the Permissions dialog box.

TIP *Always try to apply permissions to groups of users, not individual users. This reduces the need to constantly add or remove permissions for individual users. In a domain environment, make sure the user is a member of the appropriate group. In a workgroup environment, make sure the user has an account on the Web server's computer and that this account is a member of the appropriate group.*

4. Add any necessary groups.

To add a group, click the Add button. In the Add Groups dialog box (see Figure 5-31), use the Obtain List From drop-down list box to choose the computer or domain from which to get a list of groups. In the Names box, select the group you want to add, and then click the Add button. Select an option in the Allow Users To section of the dialog box to specify what level of permissions the group should be given, and then click OK.

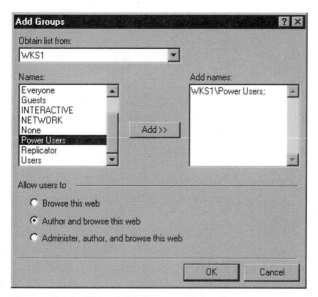

Figure 5-31 The Add Groups dialog box.

5. Edit or remove groups as necessary.

To edit the permissions given to a group, select the group and click the Edit button. In the Edit Groups dialog box, choose the permissions the group should have and then click OK. To remove a group's permissions from the FrontPage web, select the group and click the Remove button.

NOTE *You may want to remove the Everyone group and select the Only Registered Users Have Browse Access option on the Users tab to tighten up security. This gives the ability to locally browse (view) your FrontPage web to only those users that are either members of a group given browse (or higher) access or are explicitly given browse (or higher) access themselves.*

6. Add, edit, or remove users as necessary.

Click the Users tab to view the individual users explicitly given access to the FrontPage web. Use this tab just like the Groups tab, and click OK when finished to apply the new security settings to your FrontPage web.

Conducting Work with Multiple Users

After setting up FrontPage to work with multiple users, you can then check out pages to users, assign tasks to users, and view what tasks are assigned to whom.

Checking In and Checking Out Files

When many people work on a FrontPage web, it's essential for all users to check out files that they are going to modify, to prevent another user from modifying the same file at the same time.

After the check-in and check-out feature has been enabled in FrontPage (see "Enabling Document Check-In and Check-Out Capabilities" earlier in this section), it's relatively simple to check out and check in files:

- To check out a file, right-click the file in the Folder List and choose Check Out from the shortcut menu. This prevents other users from editing the file until it is checked in.

- To check in a file, right-click a checked-out file (one with a red check next to it) and choose Check In from the shortcut menu, as shown in Figure 5-32. The check-in step saves your changes and allows others to then edit the file.

- To check in a file *without saving your changes*, right-click a checked-out file and choose Undo Check Out from the shortcut menu.

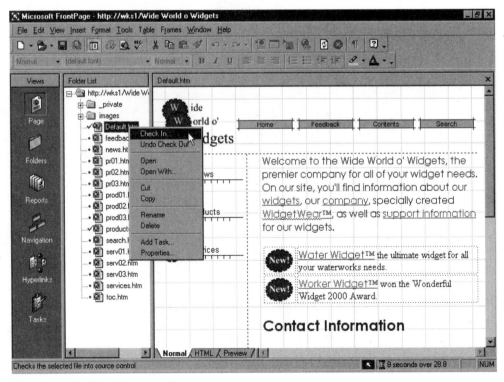

Figure 5-32 Checking in a file.

TIP *You can view the check-out status of all files on your Web site by choosing the Checkout Status report from the Reporting toolbar while in Reports view.*

Assigning Tasks

An essential part of creating a Web site with a group is assigning tasks to members of the group. This ensures that group members know which tasks they need to perform and permits the Web site creation process to go smoother and more efficiently.

Tasks are viewed and assigned using the Tasks view, which is covered earlier in the section "Using Views to View Your Web Site." They can also be viewed using the Assigned To report in the Reports view.

Changing the Category or Review Status of a File

If you want to use categories or review statuses to organize files and identify their standing in the creation process, you need to assign files to one or more categories and select a review status for the files. To do this, right-click a file in the Folder List, choose Properties from the shortcut menu, and then click the Workgroup tab, as shown in Figure 5-33. In the Available Categories box, select the categories to which you want to assign the file. In the Assigned To box, make sure the file is assigned to the correct user, and then select the current status of the file from the Review Status box. Click OK when you're finished.

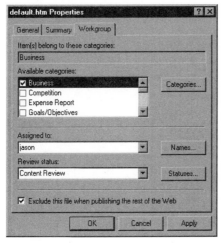

Figure 5-33 Assigning categories and a review status to a file.

TIP   *If a file needs to be reviewed before getting published to your Web site, select the Exclude This File When Publishing The Rest Of The Web check box to prevent the document from getting published to your Web site. Just remember to clear this check box when the file is ready to be published.*

TIP   *You can view files by their category or review status by using the Assigned To or Review Status reports in the Reports view. You can also see which files are excluded from publication by using the Publish Status report.*

Summary

Developing a Web site involves many tasks, including creating a FrontPage web, managing files, and creating the actual Web pages themselves. To carry out all of these tasks, it is important to thoroughly understand the FrontPage interface. This step showed you how.

In "Step 6: Polish Your Pages," you learn how to take your newly created pages and turn them into highly effective and polished pages worthy of a professional webmaster.

Step 6

POLISH YOUR PAGES

Featuring:

- Creating an Effective Home Page

- Making Your Pages Look Consistent

Creating basic Web pages in Microsoft FrontPage 2000 is straightforward and intuitive. If you can create a document in Microsoft Word, you can create a Web page in FrontPage. But to turn basic pages into pages that will hold the interest of your visitors, you need to learn some more advanced techniques. To enhance the overall look of your site, you'll need to learn how to make an effective home page, how to make your pages look consistent, and how to create tables and advanced text layouts. To help any visitors who may have trouble finding your site, you need to know how to prepare your home page for search engines.

This step shows you how to polish up your pages and improve the overall effectiveness of your Web site.

Creating an Effective Home Page

Of all the pages in your Web site, the home page (default.htm) is by far the most important. Not only is it important because it's the first page visitors see, but it also acts as a summary of the entire Web site, serves as a navigational aid, and is used by search engines to determine how to catalog your Web site. As such, an effective home page meets the following goals:

- Summarizes the content of the Web site, allowing visitors to understand at a glance what's contained on your Web site.

- Attracts visitors' interest and attention. Content is *the* most important aspect of any Web site, so it's important to showcase your best content.

- Is easy to navigate and find its information.

- Is visually appealing.

- Shows up prominently in search engines. This requires a combination of some work on the home page itself, as well as actually submitting your Web site to search engines, which is discussed in "Step 8: Deploy Your Web Site."

The following sections address these topics to make sure that your home page accomplishes all these goals.

Choosing the Best Content for Your Home Page

Deciding what content to include on your home page can be a difficult task, but a few general guidelines make it easier to determine what belongs on your home page and what belongs on other pages.

Since the home page is the first page visitors see when they come to your Web site, it's important to adequately summarize the contents of your site on the home page (this also helps your Web site place well in search engines). This doesn't mean putting a table of contents on the home page, but it does mean including hyperlinks to your major content categories. Many companies accomplish this by creating a navigation bar or set of hyperlinks, and this is an excellent way to provide a summary of what content visitors can expect to find, as well as provide them with an easy way to navigate the site. More information on creating navigation bars is presented in the "Working with Navigation Bars" section, later in this step.

Besides summarizing the content of your Web site, the home page should ideally catch the interest of visitors. One way effective Web sites do this is by having a part of the home page that features interesting content on your site or tells visitors what's new on the site.

TIP　*Regardless of what additional content you feature on your company or organization's home page, it's extremely valuable to provide direct links to the most popular content or pages on the Web site.*

If the purpose of the Web site is to advertise your company's products, feature some of your top products on the home page, with links to pages with more information. An online newsletter site might present excerpts from the newsletter's contents. A nonprofit organization might highlight its biggest projects, services, or some fact about the organization that visitors might find interesting.

Keep the content on your home page relatively short. Each featured bit of content generally shouldn't contain more than a couple lines of text or have more than one or two small images. A fine example of a Web site that provides effective, brief content on its home page is the Fortune Web site *(http://www.edf.org)*, shown in Figure 6-1. It highlights key articles and then links to other content of interest. In addition, the site is relatively clean, quick to load, and easy to understand.

Figure 6-1   A home page with well-chosen content.

Using Shared Borders to Ease Navigation

One of the best ways to implement a navigational aid for a Web s
or more shared borders on your Web site, and then place navigati
buttons in one or more of these borders. A shared border is a borc
creates along one edge of all Web pages in your Web site, and it i
put navigation bars, page titles, copyright information, and othei
might want to place in a header or footer.

NOTE   *Before the advent of shared borders, frames were a popular way of creating
common borders; however, frames have largely fallen out of favor, and shared
borders have almost entirely supplanted frames for most uses. Shared borders
are compatible with all browsers—unlike frames—and a page with shared
borders also loads slightly faster than a frames page. The only real downside
of shared borders is that they can scroll out of view with large pages; this is not
a problem with frames.*

Creating Shared Borders

To set up shared borders in your FrontPage web, you need to first tell FrontPage where
you want to place them. To do this, follow these steps:

1. **Choose the Format menu's Shared Borders command.**

    This displays the Shared Borders dialog box, as shown in Figure 6-2.

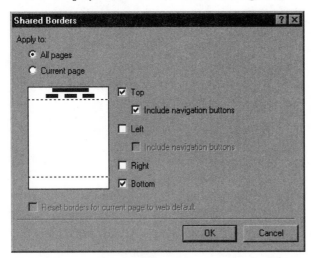

Figure 6-2   Using the Shared Borders dialog box to choose which borders to add to your
pages.

2. **Select the pages you want to have borders.**

Click the All Pages option button to apply the borders to your entire web, or click the Current Page option button to use the borders only on the current page (most likely you'll want to apply the shared borders to your entire Web site).

3. **Select the borders you want to use.**

Select the check boxes corresponding to the borders you want to add. If you want to add navigational buttons to the top and/or left border, select the appropriate Include Navigation Buttons check box. Click OK when you're finished.

Working with Navigation Bars

If you chose to include navigation buttons when you created the shared borders, a navigation bar is automatically created for you. Navigation bars are a series of buttons or hyperlinks that help visitors quickly access the most important pages on a Web site. Although you can use FrontPage to create automatically generated navigation bars anywhere on a page, they're used to their best advantage in a shared border or a frame. (This way you don't have to insert the navigation bars on each page.)

TIP   *To add a navigation bar after creating the shared borders, click the border in which you want to add the navigation bar and then choose the Insert menu's Navigation Bar command.*

To change the content or appearance of a navigation bar, simply open the Web page containing the navigation bar (Default.htm or index.htm, the home page for your Web site) and then double-click the bar to open its properties.

NOTE   *Navigation bars get their information on which pages to use from the Navigation view. Make sure any pages you want to appear on navigation bars are properly located on the Navigation view's tree.*

In the Navigation Bar Properties dialog box shown in Figure 6-3, use the section at the top of the dialog box to choose which hyperlinks to include on the navigation bar. Specify how you want your navigation bar to appear by selecting option buttons in the Orientation And Appearance section, and then click OK when you're finished.

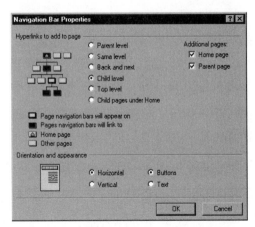

Figure 6-3 Specifying navigation bar properties.

TIP   *Figuring out which pages to include on your navigation bar(s) may initially involve a bit of head scratching. Users should be able to easily figure out where they are, where in the Web site they want to or should go next, and how to get back to where they were. This is often accomplished by selecting the Home check box, but in deep sites it may be handy to use the Child Level option in addition to selecting the Home Page and Parent Page check boxes. Regardless, you'll probably want to fiddle with these settings and test the results—ideally with some new users. See "Step 8: Deploy Your Web Site" for more information on testing Web sites.*

You can customize the text labels that appear on navigation bars in a couple ways. The text labels for pages are derived from the page titles, which appear in the Navigation view. To change these labels, change the titles of the pages. To change generic labels, such as the Home, Up, Back, or Next labels, choose the Tools menu's Web Settings command, click the Navigation tab, and change the labels to words of your choice.

TIP   *Besides using shared borders and navigation bars, it's often helpful to create smaller navigational aids for certain sections of your Web site. For example, multiple page stories can benefit from a sort of miniature Table of Contents with links to all pages in the story; and long pages can benefit from using bookmarks (hyperlinks to a different part of the same page) to improve the ability to quickly get to part of the page (although it's generally recommended to use multiple shorter pages than one long page).*

Working with Page Banners

If you create a shared border across the top of your Web pages, it usually works out well to include a page banner, which is an automatically created heading that displays the title of the page.

To add a page banner to a shared border, position the cursor inside the shared border in the appropriate location and choose the Insert menu's Page Banner command. (You can actually do this anywhere, but typically you'll insert page banners only in a shared border.) Choose an option button to specify whether you want the banner to appear as a picture with a graphic (which looks nice if you have a theme applied to the Web page) or as plain text (see Figure 6-4). Enter the banner's text in the Page Banner Text box, and click OK when you're finished.

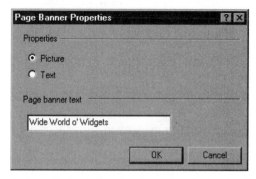

Figure 6-4   The Page Banner Properties dialog box.

TIP   *The information for each shared border is stored in a Web page located in the hidden _borders folder of your FrontPage web. To view these pages, choose the Tools menu's Options command, click the Advanced tab, and then select the Show Documents In Hidden Directories check box.*

Making Your Home Page Visually Appealing

The same techniques that make a visually appealing home page usually apply to all Web pages in general. However, here are some recommendations specifically to improve the visual appeal of your home page:

- Use an attractive company logo. If your company or organization has a logo, convert it to a GIF file and place it on your home page, perhaps in a shared border. If you do use a logo, keep it small, make sure to place it in a consistent location with a consistent size, and consider saving the logo as a transparent GIF using a stand-alone image editor so that the logo isn't outlined with a solid color. If you don't already have a company logo or one in a computer readable format, consider hiring a graphics professional to create one, or try your hand at it using a drawing program such as Microsoft PhotoDraw or Adobe Illustrator.

- Use a theme or an attractive set of colors. FrontPage ships with a large number of professionally created color and graphic schemes that you can use to give your Web site a more professional look. Unfortunately, everyone else with FrontPage has these same themes, so you run the risk of being less than unique if you use a bundled FrontPage theme. If this is a concern, consider purchasing extra themes from a third-party supplier (check *www.frontpageworld.com* for a list of suppliers), or creating or modifying a theme yourself, or with the assistance of a graphics professional.

- Don't overload your home page. It's tempting to include every last link and bit of information possible on your home page, but we strongly discourage this. An overloaded home page makes it more difficult for visitors to find the most important links and information. Choose some key elements to display, and leave the rest of the home page relatively uncluttered.

- Have good visual flow. Design your pages to attract the eye to the entire page, not just a single part of it. Be careful not to overload the home page when you do this, otherwise the eye won't be able to settle comfortably on anything.

- Make sure that your home page (and other pages on your site) don't take too long to load over a slow Internet connection. In general, pages should take less than 30 seconds to download over a 28.8Kbps modem. FrontPage gives an estimate of how long it will take to download the currently open page in the lower right side of the FrontPage's status bar, at the bottom of the screen.

Preparing Your Home Page for Search Engines

One crucial part of designing a Web site that's often overlooked is preparing your site for search engines. This includes more than just submitting your site to the most popular search engines. It also means adding some special HTML codes to your home page that tell search engines how to deal with your Web site.

These special codes are called meta tags (or meta variables), and they store information about your Web site, such as a description and keywords, that search engines use to determine when to display your Web site in a list of search results, as well as how to display your site. While not all search engines look for these tags, there are enough out there to justify including them on your home page. (Many search engines that index pages based on meta tags will nonetheless display the description you enter in your home page's description meta tag in the search results they generate.) To configure your home page with meta tags for search engines, follow these steps:

1. **Open the page properties for your home page.**

   Open your home page, and then choose Properties from the File menu. This displays the Page Properties dialog box.

2. **Click the Custom tab, and create a new User Variable.**

   On the Custom tab, click the Add button in the User Variables section of the Page Properties dialog box. This displays the User Meta Variable dialog box.

3. **Create the Keywords tag for your site.**

   In the Name box, enter the text *keywords*. In the Value box, enter all the keywords you want search engines to identify with your site, separated only by commas (see Figure 6-5). Click OK when you're finished.

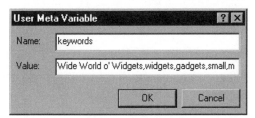

Figure 6-5   Creating the Keywords meta tag to help search engines find your site.

TIP   *Enter any common misspellings of your company or organization's name along with the rest of the keywords to enable visitors to find your site even with a spelling mistake.*

4. **Create a description User Variable for your site.**

   In the Page Properties dialog box, click the Add button in the User Variables section again to create a new User Variable to store your Web site's description. In the Name box, enter *description*. In the Value box, enter a short (25 words or less) description of your Web site. This text appears in the search results for some search engines, so it should be a concise but attractive summary of your site. Click OK when you're finished.

TIP   For more information on how search engines find pages and how to make your Web site more effective with search engines, check out http://www.searchengine.com.

Making Your Home Page Compatible with Multiple Browsers

It's very important that your home page (and other pages) be accessible to your audience, no matter what type of Web browser they're using. If your site doesn't work properly in visitors' browsers, they'll move on to some other company's Web site.

To avert this, FrontPage lets you specify with which browsers and features you want your page to be compatible. Note that changing the compatibility options removes the ability to add new features that are incompatible with the selected browser, but existing pages are unchanged, allowing them to contain incompatible features.

TIP   Even though not all FrontPage features are compatible with all browsers, you can still use many of them. Remember that some visitors won't be able to use them, so don't rely on them for something important.

To set compatibility options, follow these steps:

1. **Choose the Tools menu's Page Options command, and click the Compatibility tab.**

   This is where you can disable FrontPage commands that aren't supported by certain browsers.

2. **Choose the lowest denominator of browser you want to support.**

   In the Browsers drop-down list box, shown in Figure 6-6, select the least-capable browser you want to support on your Web site. (WebTV has the worst support for Web pages, and Netscape doesn't support all the features provided by FrontPage.)

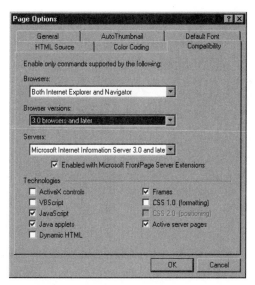

Figure 6-6   The Compatibility tab of the Page Options dialog box.

3. Choose the lowest browser version you want to support.

In the Browser Versions drop-down list box, select the oldest browser version you want to create pages for. Note that your pages will still work on older browsers, they just may have some problems or missing features.

4. Choose the type of Web server you have.

The Servers drop-down list box defaults to Microsoft Internet Information Server 3.0 and later, which is most likely what you'll be using. (This is the setting to use for all Windows 2000 or Windows NT 4 Web servers.) Select Apache if your Web server is running Linux and the Apache Web server.

5. Specify whether your Web server is using FrontPage Server Extensions.

Select the Enabled With Microsoft FrontPage Server Extensions check box if your Web server has FrontPage or Office Server Extensions installed. (Hopefully it does, otherwise consider switching to a different Web hosting company, as discussed in "Step 3: Lay a Foundation.")

6. Optionally, enable or disable individual technologies.

Use the Technologies check boxes to specify individual technologies you want to allow on your Web page. Click OK when you're finished.

TIP *Microsoft WebTV now supports some technologies that it didn't when FrontPage 2000 was created, such as JavaScript and Dynamic HTML. However, WebTV has some additional "quirks" that aren't instantly apparent, such as a fixed size 544x372 display resolution (which is somewhat lower than the lowest resolution supported by most modern computers—640x480) and the difficulty of reading fonts smaller than size 16. If you want WebTV viewers to be able to adequately view your site, check out Microsoft's WebTV developer site at* http://developer.webtv.net. *Also consider testing your site on a WebTV device, or at the very least, the viewer available on the WebTV site.*

Making Your Home Page Resolution Independent

Your Web site is going to be viewed at a large number of different screen resolutions and window sizes, so it's important that your home page (and entire site) look good at the widest range of sizes possible. Some visitors will be browsing with old computers running their display at 640x480, some will be using giant monitors at 1600x1280 resolution, and some will even be using a TV-based Web appliance, possibly running at 544x372 resolution. Figure 6-7 shows a resolution-independent Web page at 640x480 resolution, and Figure 6-8 shows the same page at a fairly typical 1024x768 resolution.

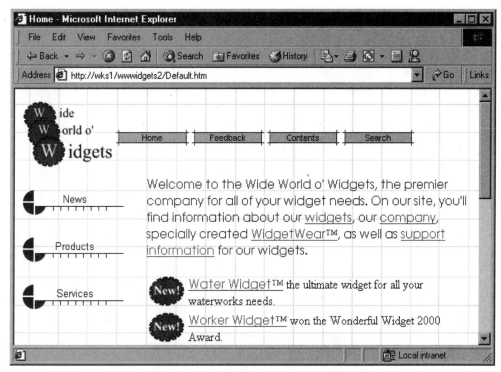

Figure 6-7 A Web page that looks good at 640x480 resolution.

Tip *Design your web pages to look good at the standard resolutions (640x480, 800x600, and 1024x768)—they'll be passable at highter resolutions, although their layout may look rather sparse. However, it is difficult and usually unnecessary to tailor your web pages to higher resolutions. Pages written for higher resolutions rarely look good at lower resolutions, and users of high screen resolutions will often use browser windows that don't encompass the full screen, often times yielding an effective window size of 1024x768.*

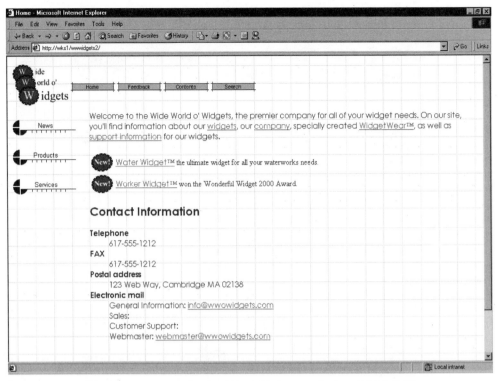

Figure 6-8   The same page, scaling well to a higher resolution (1024x768).

Here are some recommendations to help you make your site look good at all these resolutions:

- Don't overload your home page and other pages with so much content that the page is wider than a 640x480 screen. It's okay to have pages be longer in height so that users must scroll down, but users should never have to scroll from side to side.

- Make sure that your graphics aren't too wide to fit in a 640x480 screen (or 544x372 for WebTV support).

- Don't press the Enter key at the end of each line of text. FrontPage will automatically wrap lines as appropriate for a given window size *unless* you force line breaks by pressing Enter at the end of a line. Allowing FrontPage to do the line wrapping makes your pages adapt well to both higher and lower resolutions.

- When creating tables, either use the Table menu's AutoFit command to make the table sized perfectly to your content, and yet still remain flexible at different window sizes, or specify the table size in percentage, *not* in pixels.

- Size horizontal lines in percentage and not pixels, unless the width in pixels is less than 600 (even so, using percentage helps the page scale better at higher resolutions).

- Test your pages at a variety of different resolutions and window sizes. Make sure all pages look good both at high resolutions and low resolutions.

Making Your Pages Look Consistent

A Web site appears coherent and well integrated when the pages in the site are consistent in look and feel. This doesn't mean they all have to be identical. It's good to have some variation, and depending on the size of the site, you may want to have a couple different looks for your pages. But overall your site has more impact if your pages use consistent colors, graphics, and page designs.

TIP   *Two small ways to make your pages look consistent is by reusing images on different pages (which also decreases the load time for pages) and using shared borders for page banners, footers, and navigation bars.*

TIP   *Style sheets are another good way to bring consistency to pages in your site, although they are incompatible with some browsers, notably Netscape Navigator and Internet Explorer versions 3.x and earlier; Microsoft WebTV; most handheld Internet devices; and most Internet appliances, such as iOpener.*

The following sections tell you how to create templates to use for quickly creating new pages that already having the same look and feel as an existing page, format page colors and backgrounds, and apply themes to your pages.

TIP   *A technique that was pioneered on news Web sites that can be put to use on other Web sites is the related links section, usually found at the bottom of a Web page. These links enable visitors to get to other pages that feature similar content.*

Creating Templates for Often-Used Page Types

Creating templates is a great way to streamline the page creation process as well as to help give the pages on your site a consistent look. When you use a template to create a new Web page, the new page starts out looking like the template instead of being blank. If certain pages need to have the company logo, be linked to a style sheet, or use a certain layout, you can create a template that satisfies these needs. When you need to create a page with these features, the template has already taken care of these elements.

To create a template, follow these steps:

1. Create a Web page exactly how you want the template to appear.

Create a new page or open an existing one, and enter any text and images you want to appear in the template. Format the text and colors as appropriate (or link the page to a style sheet).

TIP   *If you apply a theme to a template, one of two things might happen. If the page uses the Web site's default theme, pages created with the template will also use the default theme of the FrontPage web. If a theme is applied only to the template, new pages created using the template will also use this theme, even if the web uses a different theme.*

2. Save the page as a template.

To do this, choose the File menu's Save As command, enter the name for the template in the File Name box, select FrontPage Template from the Save As Type drop-down list box, and click Save.

TIP   *Templates are saved by default to the \Documents and Settings\user\Application Data\Microsoft\FrontPage\Pages folder under Windows 2000. Windows NT and Windows 98 use slightly different paths. To determine where the template is saved, create a new template and look at the template's title bar in the FrontPage window to see its path.*

3. Describe the template.

In the Save As Template dialog box (shown in Figure 6-9), enter the title for the template. This will appear in the New dialog box when creating a new page using the template and will also be used as the new page's initial title. Enter a description for the template in the Description box, which shows up in the New dialog box. Select the Save Template In Current Web check box to make the template available only in the currently open Web (and not other Webs created on this computer). Click OK when you're finished. If any images are in the template, you're asked to decide what action to take with them. (See "Step 5: Create Your Web Site" for more information about this dialog box.)

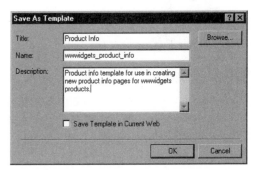

Figure 6-9   The Save As Template dialog box.

Formatting Page Colors and Backgrounds

In general, when you need to make the background information and page colors consistent across multiple pages, this information should be edited on a template. The template should then be used to create new pages, a theme should be applied, or a style sheet created and linked to all relevant documents. However, there are times when page colors and background information will need to be tweaked manually (such as to create the template), so it's useful to learn how to change these elements.

NOTE   *You cannot change a page's colors and background if the page is using a theme. See the "Using Themes" section later in this step for more information on themes.*

To manually change page colors and background information, follow these steps:

1. Choose the Format menu's Background command.

This displays the Background tab of the Page Properties dialog box, as shown in Figure 6-10, which you can use to edit the page colors and background.

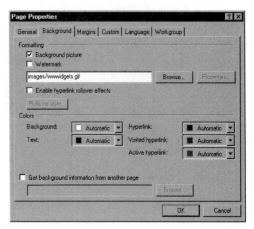

Figure 6-10 Changing the look of a page in the Page Properties dialog box.

2. Optionally, specify a background image.

To do so, select the Background Picture check box and then enter the name of the image in the text box or click the Browse button to locate the image. Select the Watermark check box to make your background image stationary when the user scrolls up or down on a page. This makes the page look as if it floats on top of the background.

TIP   *To have hyperlinks change in appearance when the user places the mouse over the link, select the Enable Hyperlink Rollover Effects check box, click the Rollover Style button, and then choose how you want the text formatting to change. This only works for visitors using Internet Explorer or Netscape 3.0 or later.*

3. Change the colors used on the Web page.

To change the colors of a page element, select the color you want from the element's drop-down list box in the Colors section.

4. Optionally, force the background information to be taken from another page.

To make a page inherit its color and background information from another page, select the Get Background Information From Another Page check box and then type the name of the page in the text box. Click OK when you're finished.

Using Themes

FrontPage includes a number of themes, which are groups of colors, graphics, and fonts that you can apply to individual Web pages or your entire web. Themes are an excellent way to apply a consistent look to the pages in your Web site, although they do lack a certain amount of uniqueness. (If this is important to you, consider purchasing a third-party theme or creating your own.)

To apply a theme to an individual page or your entire web, follow these steps:

1. **Open the page you want to modify, or select multiple pages in the Folders view.**

   To apply a theme to a single page or all pages in the FrontPage web, open a single page. To apply a theme to only certain pages, switch to Folders view and select pages by holding down the Ctrl key and clicking pages.

2. **Choose the Format menu's Themes command.**

   This displays the Themes dialog box, which you use to select a theme, modify a theme, or create a new one.

3. **Choose whether to apply the theme to all pages or only selected pages.**

   Click the All Pages option button to apply the theme to your entire web, or click the Selected Page(s) option button to apply the theme to only the currently selected pages (see Figure 6-11).

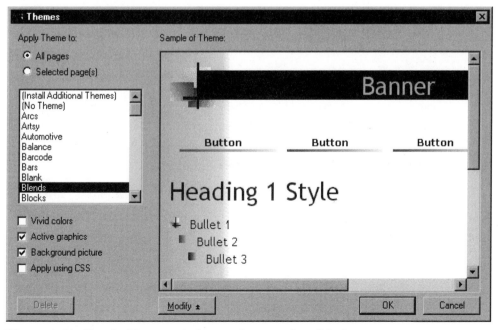

Figure 6-11 Use the Themes window to choose and modify themes.

4. Select a theme.

Choose a theme from the list, and examine the preview in the Sample Of Theme box on the right.

5. Select any minor theme options.

Select the Vivid Colors and Active Graphics check boxes to make the colors and graphics stand out more. Select the Background Picture check box to include the Theme's background picture in your pages. Select the Apply Using CSS check box to use Cascading Style Sheets to create the theme. (This feature allows you to manually edit the CSS file if you want to, but it is generally not recommended because of compatibility issues with Netscape Navigator 4.5 or earlier.)

6. Modify or create a new theme.

To modify the theme or create your own theme, click the Modify button, and then use the Colors, Graphics, and Style buttons and dialog boxes to modify the theme. To save your theme, click the Save As button.

7. Click OK to apply the theme.

FrontPage will inform you that applying a theme erases all custom font colors, background information, and fonts. Click OK to continue. Depending on how many pages you applied the theme to, FrontPage may take a bit of time to apply the theme. The theme won't be visible on your pages during this process.

TIP   *To remove a theme, select No Theme from the list of Themes, click OK, and then click the Refresh button to update your display.*

Tables and Advanced Text Layout

Tables are incredibly useful for creating advanced layouts in a Web page, and are used much more often than most people realize. Besides their obvious use for creating tables of text and graphics, tables are often used to make more precise text and graphic layouts than can be accomplished simply with standard techniques.

FrontPage supports creating and modifying tables in almost the same way that Microsoft Word does, so if you're a Word user, you'll find it easy to work with tables in FrontPage.

Besides tables, FrontPage supports several other methods of creating advanced layouts. The Format menu's Position command provides the ability to more naturally wrap text around images and tables, as well as the ability to absolutely position objects onscreen with pixel-precise accuracy. (Absolute positioning is tricky to use while remaining resolution independent, however, and using the Position command creates layouts that are only compatible with Internet Explorer and Netscape Navigator 4.0 browsers and later.) You can also modify the nitty-gritty details of bulleted and numbered lists by selecting them and choosing the Format menu's Bullets And Numbering command. In fact, the Format menu contains a wealth of formatting options that can be used to tweak your text and layouts.

TIP   *Another tool that professional Web developers use when creating advanced layouts is transparent GIF images. Create a small, completely transparent GIF image, and then use it to fill the space that you want to appear blank. If the image isn't quite the right size, resize it using the Image Properties dialog box. (There's no need to resample.) Remember that white space on a page can be very effective in leading the eye to important content and averting the possibility of overwhelming visitors with too many visual stimuli.*

Creating Tables

You can create a table by using the Insert Table toolbar button or by using the Draw Table tool, which in FrontPage is located at the top of the Table menu.

To create a table using the Insert Table toolbar button, position the cursor where you want to insert the table, click the Insert Table toolbar button, highlight the number of cells you want the table to have, and then click the lower rightmost cell to create the table, as shown in Figure 6-12.

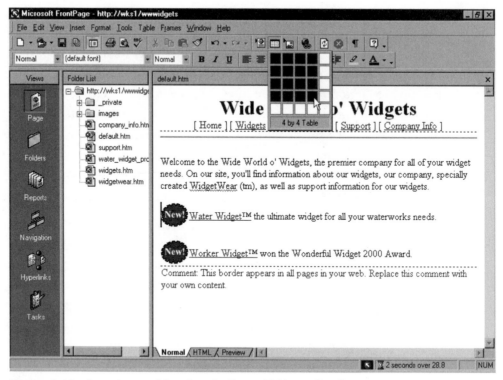

Figure 6-12   Inserting a table using the Insert Table toolbar button.

To create a table using the Draw Table tool, which allows you to draw your table free-hand, follow these steps:

1. Choose the Table menu's Draw Table command.

This displays the Table toolbar and turns the cursor into a pencil that you can use to draw the outline of your table.

2. Draw the outline for the table.

Click and drag with the Draw Table pencil to create the outline for your table. When you release the mouse button, the outer borders of the table are created.

3. Draw the dividers for the table.

Draw the dividing lines for the table by drawing a line from one side of the new table to the other in any direction, as shown in Figure 6-13.

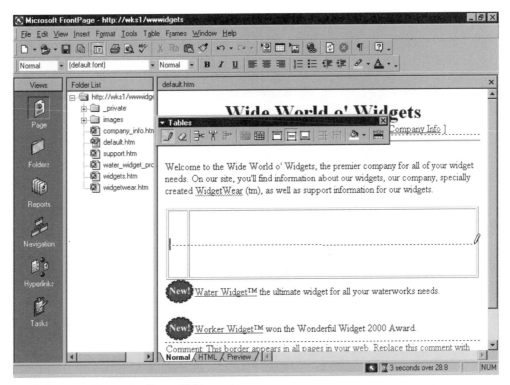

Figure 6-13 Using the Draw Table tool.

TIP   *If you make a mistake drawing dividers, click the Eraser button on the Table toolbar and erase the divider. To resize the columns or rows, move the mouse over a dividing line until the cursor turns into a dual-sided arrow, and then drag the divider to the desired location.*

4. Add content to the table.

Add content to the table by entering text or inserting images, or select a block of text or an image and drag it into a table cell to move the text or image into the new table.

Modifying Table Properties

The tables that FrontPage creates usually require a little tweaking before they can be put to use on a company or organization's Web site. For example, if you're using the table to position text more precisely, you'll probably want to make the table invisible (by eliminating the table borders). Or you may need to adjust the sizing of the table, how it's aligned on the page, or the colors or background image used. To do so, follow these steps:

1. **Right-click the table, and choose Table Properties from the shortcut menu.**

   This displays the Table Properties dialog box, shown in Figure 6-14, which you can use to adjust all the details of your table.

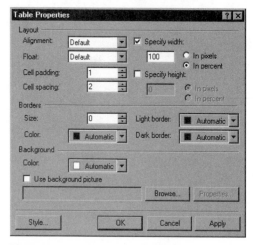

Figure 6-14 Using the Table Properties dialog box to change a table's appearance.

2. **Specify how the table should be aligned on the page.**

   Select an entry from the Alignment drop-down list box to specify how the table should be aligned on the page.

3. **Choose on which side of the table the text should wrap.**

   To allow text and other objects on your page to be displayed next to the table, select an entry from the Float drop-down list box to specify on which side of the table that text and images should be allowed.

4. **Specify the cell padding and spacing.**

   In the Cell Padding box, specify how many pixels you want between the contents of a cell and the cell border. In the Cell Spacing box, enter the width in pixels of the table border.

5. **Manually specify the width and height of the table.**

   To manually control the width and height of the table, select the Specify Width and/ or Specify Height check boxes and then enter the width or height of the table in percent or in pixels.

Specify the size of your table in percent rather than in pixels if you want your table to scale well to a different window size or screen resolution. The Table menu's AutoFit command is also a useful way of creating a table that sizes perfectly to your content and also appears properly at different screen resolutions.

6. Specify the thickness of the table's lines.

In the Size box of the Borders section, enter the desired thickness in pixels of the table's dividing lines. You can also use the Color, Light Border, and Dark Border boxes to change the colors used to draw the dividing lines.

TIP *Set the border thickness to zero to hide all lines in a table, only showing the contents. This is one of the most often used layout tricks on the Web, so it's worth learning.*

7. Optionally, select a background color or image for the table.

Select a background color for your table from the Color drop-down list box in the Background section, or select the Use Background Picture check box and type the name of the image you want to use in the text box provided. Click OK when you're finished.

NOTE *Only Internet Explorer 3.0 and newer versions support using background pictures in a table. Currently Netscape Navigator and WebTV don't support this feature.*

Specifying Cell Properties

You can change the properties of individual cells or a group of cells, such as a column or row, separately from the rest of the table. This is useful if you want the contents of particular cells to be aligned differently, or perhaps if you want to set some cells apart by giving them a different colored background. (This feature can also be used with invisible tables to create a visual divider in a page, without the actual table showing up.)

To change the appearance of an individual cell, follow these steps:

1. Select the cell(s) you want to modify, and open the cell properties.

Right-click inside the cell you want to modify, and then choose Cell Properties from the shortcut menu.

TIP   *To select multiple cells, position the cursor in a cell, choose the Table menu's Select->Cell command, and then click any other cells you want to select.*

2. Modify the cell properties.

The properties of a cell are no different from those of the table as a whole (see the previous section), except for a couple of special options, as shown in Figure 6-15. Select the Header Cell check box if the cell is a header for the table. (This makes the cell's contents boldface.) Select the No Wrap check box to force all the text inside a cell to remain on one line, no matter how small the window size gets. (This is useful for text that absolutely cannot wrap, but use it sparingly.) Click OK when you're finished.

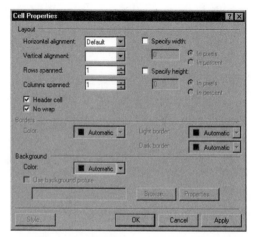

Figure 6-15 Using the Cell Properties dialog box to specify how a cell should appear.

Summary

In this step we showed you some specific techniques you can use to make your Web pages more effective. This included ways to sharpen up your home page, such as improving site navigation and visual appeal, as well as how to make all the pages in your Web site consistent in appearance, and how to create tables and advanced text layouts.

In "Step 7: Add Interactivity to Your Web Site," we introduce forms, describe Web-based discussion groups, and outline options for setting up a Web store on your site.

ADD INTERACTIVITY TO YOUR WEB SITE

Featuring:

- Working with Forms

- Creating a Search Form

- Creating Web-Based Discussions

- Creating Web Stores

The ability to collect information from Web site visitors can be a powerful business tool. You can use forms to collect survey or ordering information from users or create a search form for your Web site. Additionally, Microsoft FrontPage 2000 makes it relatively easy to create discussion forums on your site.

Unfortunately, FrontPage 2000 does *not* make it easy to create Web sites with integrated Web stores and credit card processing. This step introduces forms and discussion forums and also presents some options that are available should you decide to create an online storefront for your company or organization.

NOTE   *Your company or organization may not require interactivity on its Web site. We recommend that you avoid adding such advanced features until after you have a simple Web site up and running.*

Working with Forms

The most effective method of obtaining information from visitors is through a form on your Web site. In the past, creating forms was an arduous task requiring HTML coding and special CGI scripts. You can now avoid this hassle and easily create forms visually within FrontPage, provided that your Web host supports FrontPage Server Extensions.

NOTE *You can create forms using FrontPage for Web sites that don't support FrontPage Server Extensions, although you will have to interface the forms with the CGI scripts on your Web server, which takes some additional effort. Inquire with your Web hosting company as to the proper procedure to do this.*

We recommend that you read over our suggestions for creating effective forms before you actually begin creating your forms. Once you've gotten a better idea of how to create forms that accomplish your goals, we walk you through creating forms, working with form fields, and modifying form properties.

Creating Effective Forms

People don't like to fill out forms. Because of this basic facet of human psychology, we recommend that you strive to make your forms easy and painless for visitors to complete. Here are some recommendations for creating successful forms on your Web site:

- Limit the number of forms you create on your site. In general, it's difficult to get visitors to complete a single form, and almost impossible to get them to fill out multiple unrelated forms. (Stages of a registration or order process are an exception.)

- Keep your forms short. When presented with a long form, many visitors will move on. Short forms are much more palatable. In fact, placing a one- or two-question survey form on a Web page can be enticing to visitors, especially if the results of the survey are shown. Although these one-question forms may not always provide much information to your company or organization, they can be a way to make visitors feel a better sense of community on the site. (The site *www.drweil.com* makes good use of this technique, as shown in Figure 7-1.)

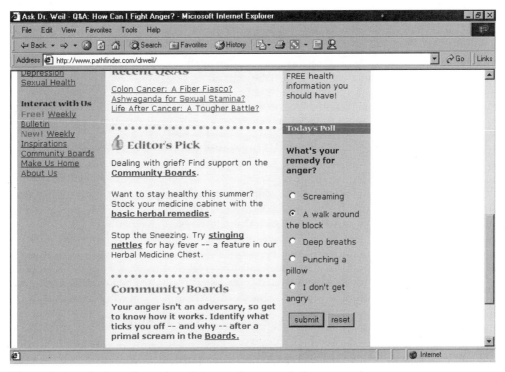

Figure 7-1 A short form that visitors enjoy completing.

NOTE *Automatically processing submitted data and displaying it as the current results of a running survey isn't very easy. It usually involves submitting form data to a database and then creating a Web page that queries this database and displays the results. However, it isn't difficult to collect all the information into a text file, import the text file into Microsoft Excel, create a chart of the data, and then post that chart on your Web site the next week. The results aren't immediately available, but this system is much easier to implement, and some visitors might respond to the incentive and return to your site at a later time.*

- Clearly mark which fields, if any, are required. Many visitors will skip questions they don't want to answer. Marking which fields your visitors are required to complete saves them the frustration of being forced to go back and fill out skipped fields.

- Leave as many fields optional as possible. Visitors are more likely to fill out longer forms if some of the fields are left optional (allowing visitors to, in essence, choose the length of the form they want to fill out).

- Validate any important text fields to reduce the chance of collecting incorrect data. You can configure form fields to check that input is correct. For example, if you're asking for a phone number, you can check to make sure that only numbers were entered and not letters or other characters.

- Ask for personal information only when necessary. People are very wary of giving out any personal information on the Internet, including their e-mail address, and will oftentimes avoid any forms asking for such information.

- When asking for personal information, clearly state your privacy policy. You can assuage visitors' privacy concerns by clearly and succinctly stating what you will do with the information they provide. If the form is designed to add users to a mailing list, assure your visitors that you won't share their e-mail address with anyone else.

- Ask for credit card information only over a secure (SSL) connection. Any moderately sophisticated hacker can intercept credit card information that is submitted using a form on a nonsecure Web site. The solution is to handle credit card information only on a secure Web site—that is, a site that has been SSL enabled and starts with the prefix *https://* instead of *http://*. (See the "Creating Web Stores" section later in this step for more information.)

- Collect credit card information at the last possible moment. If you are collecting credit card information (over a secure connection), make sure that it's the last phase of the ordering process. For example, make sure that you clearly inform visitors of all costs involved, including tax and shipping and handling, before they are required to give out their credit card information.

Creating Forms Pages

FrontPage comes with a couple of form page templates and a Form Page Wizard to help you get started creating forms. To create a new page with a form, choose the File menu's New command, and then choose Page from the submenu. Choose the Form Page Wizard or a form page template from the list box, and then click OK (see Figure 7-2).

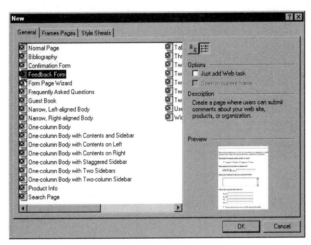

Figure 7-2   Choosing a Form Page template or wizard to create a new page containing a form.

Inserting Form Fields

To insert a new form field (such as a drop-down menu or a check box) into your form, place your cursor where you want to add the form field, choose the Insert menu's Form command, and then choose the type of field you want to insert from the submenu, as shown in Figure 7-3.

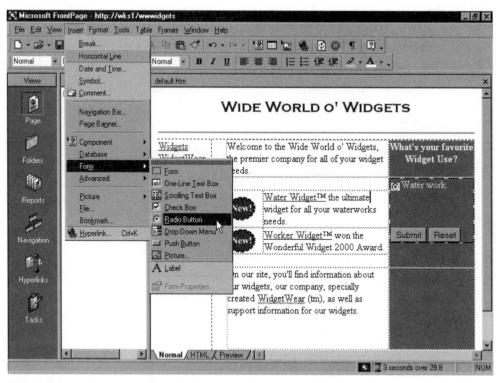

Figure 7-3　Choosing a form field to insert.

TIP　*You can insert a form field into any page. When you insert a form field outside of a form, FrontPage automatically constructs a form for the field to go in. You can then work with the form like any other form.*

Modifying Form Field Properties

FrontPage does a passable job of configuring form fields when you insert them into a form; however, most companies and organizations will find it desirable to modify the fields somewhat to more accurately reflect the information the form is gathering. While each form field's properties are slightly different, the following procedure walks you through modifying the properties of form fields in enough detail to help you understand most of the user configurable properties of each form field type:

1. Open the form field's properties.

Right-click the field you want to modify, and then choose Form Field Properties (not Form Properties) from the shortcut menu.

2. Name the field or group.

Enter a short but descriptive name for the field in the Name box, as shown in Figure 7-4. If you created a radio button (also known as an option button), enter the name you want to use for the group of buttons in the Group Name box. Since radio buttons are intended to represent options that a user can select, they must be placed in a group, and only one button in a group can be selected at a time. Therefore, enter the same group name for each button you want to belong to the same group.

Figure 7-4   Naming a text box form field.

TIP   *Field names must start with a letter and can contain upper and lowercase letters, numbers, and the underscore character. All other characters, including spaces, are prohibited.*

3. Enter a value for the field.

Enter a short and descriptive value for the field. For example, you might use the no_mail value for a check box allowing visitors to request not to receive any e-mail from you. For text boxes, optionally enter any text you want to be initially present in the box (users can change it as they choose). A button is a little different because its value doubles as the button's label.

TIP   *The names and values you choose will not usually appear on the forms themselves (except for button and drop-down menu values); however, they will appear on the confirmation page that visitors see after they submit a form. If you change FrontPage's names and values to reflect the actual meaning of the form field, visitors can better understand what they submitted when they read the confirmation page.*

NOTE *Check boxes, radio buttons, and buttons are all binary form fields—they're either on or off. When they're on (selected or pushed), they send the contents of the Value box to the form handler (the software that gathers data from the form). The form handler displays this information on the confirmation page and in the form results (which you'll view by Web page, text document, or e-mail). For text boxes, the visitor enters the value when he or she types in the text box, although you can set an initial value if you want.*

4. Choose the initial state of the field.

If the form field has two states (selected or not selected), use the Initial State options or check boxes to select the way you want the form field to initially appear to a visitor.

NOTE *Drop-down menus work a little differently from the other form fields. To add a choice to a drop-down menu, click the Add button in the Drop-Down Menu Properties dialog box. Then enter the text (value) you want to appear as a choice on the menu in the Add Choice dialog box, and choose whether the choice should be initially selected or not. You can then use the Drop-Down Menu Properties dialog box to move choices around on the menu and control whether to allow multiple menu selections or not.*

5. Enter the tab order for the field.

Visitors can switch between form fields using the Tab key on their keyboard. To control the order in which form fields are reached using the Tab key; enter a unique number in the Tab Order box for each form field. Pressing the tab key will cycle through the form fields, starting with the field containing a 1 in the Tab Order box. If you leave the Tab Order boxes empty, the fields will be accessed in the order in which they appear on the page.

TIP *To exclude a form field from the tab order, enter –1 in the Tab Order box.*

6. Optionally, validate the form field.

If you want to require that the form field is used, or if you want to validate the data the user entered, click the Validate button in the form field's Properties dialog box. This is especially useful for text boxes, where you may want to ensure that the visitor entered the correct type of data. For example, if you have a telephone number field, set up the field to validate that the user entered Text in the Digits format (see Figure 7-5). This allows numbers and dashes, but no letters or other characters. If you require that users enter their phone number, specify a minimum Data Length of 10 characters so that you're assured users will enter their area code in addition to their phone number.

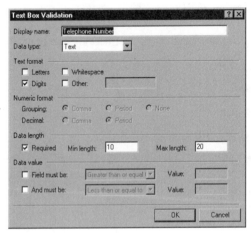

Figure 7-5   Validating a text box form field.

Modifying Form Properties

Besides modifying the properties of individual form fields, you'll probably find it useful to change the way that the form handles submitted data. For example, you might want information to be automatically e-mailed to a certain e-mail address or perhaps written to a text file for eventual data analysis in a spreadsheet or database program.

To modify the properties for a form, follow these steps:

1. Open the form's properties.

Right-click anywhere in your form, and then choose Form Properties from the shortcut menu to display the Form Properties dialog box.

2. Enter the filename of the location where you want to store form results.

Enter the filename where you want form results stored, in the File Name text box, as shown in Figure 7-6.

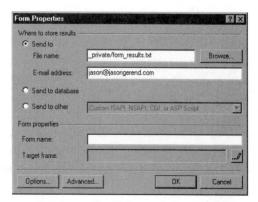

Figure 7-6 Specifying where FrontPage should store the results from your form.

3. Optionally, specify an e-mail address where form results can be sent.

To automatically send all form submissions to an e-mail address, enter the e-mail address that you want form results sent to in the E-Mail Address text box.

4. Modify advanced options, if desired.

Click the Options button to modify the form's advanced options. For example, to change the file format for the form results file, choose an option from the File Format drop-down list box in the Options For Saving Results Of Form dialog box (see Figure 7-7). Click the E-Mail Results tab to modify the e-mail format and the subject line for results that are e-mailed to someone. Click the Saved Fields tab to specify what form fields should be saved and to specify additional information to save, such as browser type.

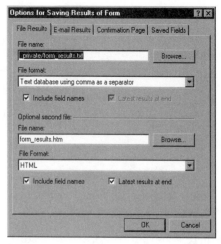

Figure 7-7 Changing the file format for the form results file.

FrontPage automatically generates a confirmation page displaying the information submitted on a form. You can use your own confirmation page by clicking the Confirmation Page tab in the Options For Saving Results Of Form dialog box and entering the name of the page in the text box. In your confirmation page, use the Insert menu's Component->Confirmation Field command to insert confirmation fields corresponding to the fields you want to confirm.

Creating a Search Form

A search form is a special type of form that allows visitors to search for information on your Web site. Usually search forms are complicated to create and involve a certain amount of scripting, but FrontPage provides a special Search Form component that you can use to quickly and easily create a working search form on your site.

NOTE *To use FrontPage's search form component on your Web site, your Web hosting company's Web server needs to support FrontPage Server Extensions. Also, its server needs to be configured to properly search your site, which may require some additional configuration on the part of the Web host. Consult with your Web hosting provider for more details.*

To insert a form that visitors can use to search for a particular page on your Web site, follow these steps:

1. Insert the Search Form component.

Position the cursor where you want to insert your search form, click the Insert Component toolbar button, and then choose Search Form from the drop-down menu.

TIP *You can create a dedicated search page by creating a new page using the Search Page template.*

2. Create a label for the search form.

Type a label for the search form in the Label For Input text box (see Figure 7-8).

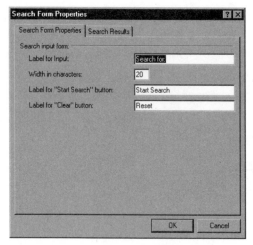

Figure 7-8 Changing the properties for a search form.

3. Specify the width of your search field.

Use the Width In Characters text box to specify how many characters that visitors are allowed to enter in the search field.

4. Label the Start Search and Clear buttons.

If you want to change the search and reset buttons for your search form, enter new labels for the Start Search and Clear buttons in the next two text boxes.

5. Specify where the search form should look for pages.

Click the Search Results tab (as shown in Figure 7-9), and then specify what parts of the Web site the search form should search. Most companies and organizations will want their entire site searched, although if a subweb contains the search form, you might want to search only the subweb by clicking the This Web option button. To search a particular directory, click the Directory option button and enter the directory name in the box provided.

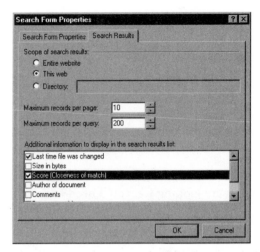

Figure 7-9   Specifying how you want search results displayed.

6. Modify how search results are displayed.

Use the Maximum Records Per Page and Maximum Records Per Query boxes to specify how many matching pages should be listed per page, and the maximum number of matching Web pages the search form should locate. Use the check boxes at the bottom of the dialog box to display additional information about matching pages, and click OK when you're finished.

TIP   *If you want to test your search form locally before publishing it to your Web hosting company's Web server, your local Web server will need to be specially configured. This is simple on Windows 2000 Web servers; see the Appendix "Set Up Your Web Site on a Local Web Server" for more information.*

Creating Web-Based Discussions

Discussion groups can add another element of interactivity to your Web site, providing users with a valuable source of information that's of interest to them. They can serve as forums in which visitors can ask questions that aren't specific to customer support or share tips and stories about your products and services or subjects related to them. Discussion groups also build a sense of community within your site. They are one more way to keep visitors coming back frequently to your Web site.

There are two ways of developing a discussion group on your Web site: you can set up a live chat system or create a newsgroup-like discussion board.

Discussion groups can also be a valuable tool that a business or organization can use for its own employees. By creating a restricted access discussion group, employees can carry on discussions over the Web about current projects. Taken one step further, an entire project Web site can be created for employees, allowing them to view important files, post new files, and carry on discussions.

Chat-Based Discussions

FrontPage has no built-in means of creating any sort of real-time chat capabilities on a Web site, so if this is a capability you are looking for, you'll need to turn to a third-party solution. Humanclick *(www.humanclick.com)* provides one type of free chat software that allows you to conduct one-on-one chat sessions with your visitors. (This is appropriate for customer support, but it doesn't allow visitors to chat with each other.)

To set up a chat room where multiple visitors can chat with each other, you could use a free service such as Parachat *(www.parachat.com)* that displays ads at the bottom of the chat room to support the service. Or you could pay to use such a service without the ads, although this is rarely cost-effective because of the high monthly costs. (A fee of $50 per month is fairly typical for a small chat site.)

Creating Discussion Groups

Although FrontPage doesn't support chat rooms, it does support newsgroup-style discussion groups, which are generally more useful for a company or organization's Web site anyway. Using the FrontPage Discussion Web Wizard, you can create a new FrontPage web which you can link to from your existing web that allows users to post comments, read and reply to posted comments, and search for posted comments. To do so, follow these steps:

1. **Start the Discussion Web Wizard.**

   Choose the File menu's New command, and choose Web from the submenu. In the New dialog box, as shown in Figure 7-10, choose the Discussion Web Wizard. Then enter the location where you want to store this new web, or select the Add To Current Web check box to make the discussion web a part of the current FrontPage web. Click OK.

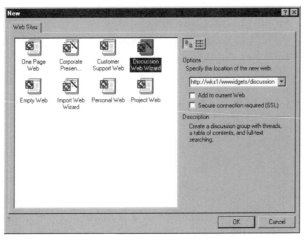

Figure 7-10 Choosing the Discussion Web Wizard.

TIP *Create your discussion group as a web separate from your existing web for maximum flexibility in creating and modifying the discussion group. The best way to do this is to create the discussion web in a subfolder of your existing web. For example, if your existing web were stored locally at http://wks1/mycompany, you would create your discussion web at http://wks1/mycompany/discussion.*

2. Specify the features you want.

Click Next in the first screen of the wizard, and then select the features you want your discussion group to have, as shown in Figure 7-11. Click Next to continue.

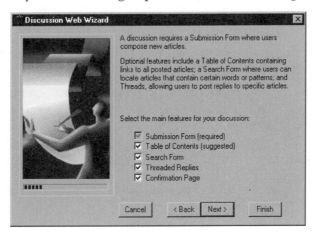

Figure 7-11 Selecting which discussion features to include.

3. Name the discussion group.

In the next screen of the wizard, enter a name for the discussion group in the first box provided. In the second box, enter a name for the hidden folder in your Web site that will store the actual discussion articles, and then click Next.

4. Choose which fields to include on the posting form.

Comments are posted to the discussion group using a form that FrontPage creates. Select which fields to include on this form, and then click Next.

5. Specify whether to restrict access to the discussion group.

FrontPage is capable of restricting access to the discussion group, allowing only users who have registered and obtained a username and password to join the group. If you want to restrict access, click the Yes, Only Registered Users Are Allowed option button. Otherwise, click the No, Anyone Can Post Articles option button, and then click Next.

WARNING *If your Web hosting company uses a Microsoft Web server (Internet Information Server), users will not be able to create their own username and password for your Web site. In order to maintain a secure Web site, you will need to manually create user accounts on the Web server for each user. (This is typically done through a special Web page on your Web hosting company's Web site. Consult your Web host for additional information.)*

NOTE *In order to create a restricted discussion group, you need to change the security settings for the FrontPage web to allow only registered users Browse Access. Because of this, restricted discussion groups must be created as subwebs or entirely separate FrontPage webs.*

6. Choose how articles should be sorted.

If you chose to include a Table of Contents for the discussion group, FrontPage asks whether it should sort articles from oldest to newest or from newest to oldest. Although the default is oldest to newest, many prefer to see the newest articles displayed first, so consider selecting the Newest To Oldest option. Click Next to continue.

7. Choose whether to make the Table of Contents the home page for this web.

If you chose to create an entirely new FrontPage web for the discussion group, select Yes when asked if you want the Table of Contents to be the home page for this web. Otherwise, select No to avoid having your existing home page overwritten, and then click Next.

8. **Modify the search form for the discussion group.**

If you chose to include a search form for the discussion group, select which information the search form should display for matching discussion posts that it locates, and then click Next.

9. **Choose the interface.**

Through the use of frames, FrontPage can allow users to view the Table of Contents and an article at the same time. Select the layout you want to use, and then click Next, as shown in Figure 7-12. Click Finish to create your discussion group.

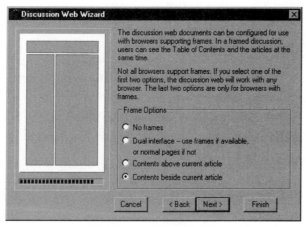

Figure 7-12 Choosing a layout for your discussion group.

NOTE   *If you select a frame option other than No Frames or Dual Interface, visitors with a Web browser incapable of displaying frames won't be able to use your discussion groups. This usually isn't much of an issue, since almost all browsers support frames. However, some information appliances don't, so if this is a concern, consider using the Dual Interface option.*

10. **Edit pages as necessary.**

After FrontPage creates your discussion group, you'll probably want to edit some of the pages, such as the disc_welc.htm page—the welcome page to the discussion group. Edit and save the pages as you would any other page in your FrontPage web.

TIP *To remove or edit posted messages (perhaps because of inappropriate remarks), first open the FrontPage web directly on your Web hosting company's Web server. (Enter your domain name in the Open Web dialog box; see "Step 5: Create Your Web Site" for information on opening webs.) Then choose the Tools menu's Web Setting command, click the Advanced tab, and select the Show Documents In Hidden Directories check box. This displays the hidden directory that you named in step 3 above, where all articles are located. Open the tocproto.htm file to help locate the article in question, and then open the article manually.*

Creating Web Stores

Web-based storefronts are extremely popular and very enticing to many companies and organizations. Unfortunately, determining how to go about setting up a Web store is an involved and potentially expensive process. FrontPage 2000 doesn't provide any remedy for this situation because it contains no real ability to easily create a Web store.

However, it is possible for a small or medium-size business or organization to set up a Web store, and the following sections describe some of your options. A brief primer outlines what's involved in creating a Web store and explains why the process is so complicated.

How Web Stores Work

There are many ways to create a Web-based store—from providing a simple product catalog and order form that visitors can print out and mail in to the full-fledged e-commerce solutions that companies such as Amazon.com and Buy.com have made everyday sights on the Web. Because these fully integrated online stores are what most businesses and companies think of when discussing e-commerce, it's useful to understand what is involved in these stores and why they are so complex and expensive to set up and maintain. The following two sections detail a typical Web-based order from the perspective of the shopper and then from the perspective of the Web server, describing what technologies are used.

What the Shopper Sees

To begin with, a visitor is presented with an online catalog of products and services that he or she can look through (such as the one shown in Figure 7-13).

Figure 7-13 Buy.com's online product catalog.

When the visitor finds a product to purchase, he or she clicks an Add To Shopping Cart or similarly named link, which adds the product to a virtual shopping cart, as shown in Figure 7-14. The shopping cart displays all the products that the visitor has picked out, the prices, and a total price, usually with shipping and tax included. Ideally, the shopping cart also displays whether or not the products are in stock.

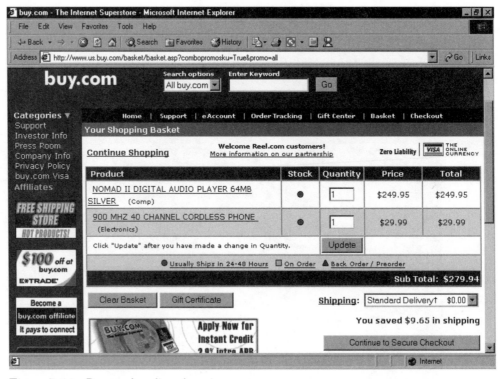

Figure 7-14 Buy.com's online shopping cart.

After the shopper has reviewed the items, he or she may then purchase the items by clicking the Continue To Secure Checkout or a similarly named link. At this point, a secure Web page is displayed prompting the shopper for billing and shipping information, including a credit card number. When the shopper is finished completing the form, he or she clicks a Submit Order button that then processes the order and displays an order confirmation showing that the order was placed.

What the Web Server Does

Behind the scenes of the above-described order process a number of things must happen, involving several different Web site technologies and techniques.

The online catalog is the simplest part. It can consist of a series of standard Web pages, such as those you create in FrontPage. However, the process gets more complicated as soon as the visitor wants to add items to a shopping cart.

To handle a shopping cart, the Web site needs to keep track of each visitor and what items he or she is placing in the shopping cart. This can be done a number of ways, but usually involves maintaining a database that exists solely to keep track of what items are placed in the shopping cart. Since FrontPage 2000 doesn't provide any shopping cart component, you need to use a third-party shopping cart system in order to do this. (This is discussed in greater detail in the "Using a Shopping Cart System" section later in this step.)

In order for the shopping cart to display the current stocking information of the products, it must be tied to your business's inventory database. This takes a significant amount of database programming and a substantial amount of configuration.

To collect the shopper's billing and shipping information, a simple form is used on a secure Web server (which your Web hosting company can provide for additional cost or as part of your Web hosting plan). This form takes the order information (which is encrypted for security) and passes along the payment information, such as the credit card number and how much to charge to the account, to a credit card processing company or bank. The bank then charges the shopper's account and credits your company's Internet Merchant account for the amount of the purchase, minus a transaction percentage and fee. The form also enters the information into your ordering database (which is ideally the same as your inventory database), which your company then queries to see what orders it needs to fill and how to fill them.

E-Commerce Options for Your Company

Now that you have a better idea what is involved with a full e-commerce solution, we can better describe the options that are available to you and which ones might make the most sense for your company.

Your company can set up a Web-based store using one of three methods: the noninteractive method, which is no different from a print catalog; the basic online order form method; and the full-fledged shopping cart method, with or without credit card processing.

Creating a Noninteractive Catalog

The easiest way to allow visitors to order products from your company is to create an online version of your print catalog and include your phone number or an order form that visitors can print out and then mail or fax to your company. This is extremely simple to do. You can use FrontPage to create your online product catalog just as you would any other page, making sure to include each product's price as well as your company's telephone number. To allow visitors to mail or fax orders to your company, you can take your existing order form and convert it into a Web page (or re-create it from scratch) or, optionally, an Adobe Acrobat file (although we recommend creating an HTML document instead). You can then place this order form on your Web site for visitors to print out and return to you via mail or fax.

Using a Secure Form to Collect Orders

A slightly more sophisticated approach to online stores is to create an order form hosted on a secure Web site to collect customer orders. This approach isn't as elegant as a shopping cart; however, it can provide a secure means of accepting orders with credit card information, and it is still relatively simple to create using FrontPage.

Credit card information is collected using the order form you create; orders are processed by manually downloading them from your Web site and then using a standard credit card reader to process the transaction. For small businesses, this method is much more cost-effective than dealing with online credit card processing, which almost universally costs more than processing credit card transactions offline using a standard credit card reader. However, some Web hosting companies will include a free shopping cart system with Web hosting plans that provide secure connections. If this is the case with your Web hosting company, you'll probably want to use it instead of the method described below.

To create a secure online order form, follow these steps:

1. **Create your online catalog.**

   Create a catalog of products or services in FrontPage as you would any other Web site or series of pages, making sure to include pricing information.

2. **Create an order form.**

   Create an order form by creating a new page using the Form Page Wizard. In the second screen of the wizard, click the Add button, and then select Ordering Information from the list in the next screen. Use the rest of the wizard to create a form already configured to collect order information. A sample form created using the wizard is shown in Figure 7-15.

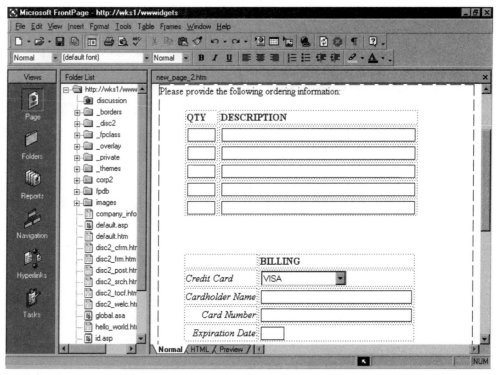

Figure 7-15   A basic order form created using the Form Page Wizard.

3. Configure the form properties.

Right-click inside the form, and choose Form Properties from the shortcut menu to modify the properties of the order form. Make sure that the form results are stored in the _private/ directory, as shown in Figure 7-16, so that only you can view orders that have been placed.

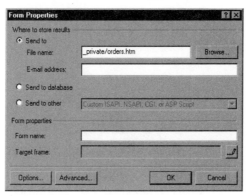

Figure 7-16   Changing the location in which form results are stored.

WARNING *Do not send form results to an e-mail address if your form is collecting credit card information. Nonencrypted e-mail is not a secure medium and should never be used for sending credit card information.*

4. Link your catalog to your order form.

Create a hyperlink in your catalog to your new order form using the secure Web site alias provided by your Web hosting company. Usually this will be in the form of *https://www.myhostingcompany.com/mycompany/order_form.htm*.

NOTE *Web hosting companies usually configure a secure alias to your Web site, for example,* https://www.myhostingcompany.com/mycompany/anypage.htm. *The alias allows you to securely access any page on your site. For specifics, contact your Web hosting company.*

5. Retrieve orders.

To retrieve the orders placed using the form, open your FrontPage web directly using the secure alias. To do this, choose the File menu's Open Web command and then enter the secure URL provided by your Web hosting company (see Figure 7-17), for example, *https://www.myhostingcompany.com/mycompany*. After your Web site is open in FrontPage, go to the _private/ directory and open your form results page to retrieve a list of orders placed since you last emptied the form results file.

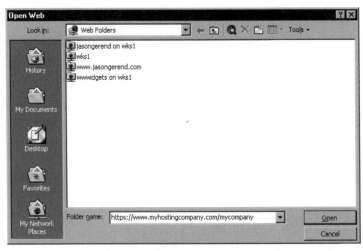

Figure 7-17 Opening your Web site using a secure connection.

NOTE *Because it's unwise to send form results containing credit card information over e-mail, you will need to regularly check your form results to see whether orders have been placed.*

6. Process the orders.

Use your credit card reader to process any credit card orders, and fill your orders as appropriate to your company.

TIP   *One way of processing the orders that are contained in your form results page is to save the page onto your hard drive and take the order information from this file instead of the form results page on your Web site. You can then safely delete the contents of the form results page on your Web site to reduce the risk of processing an order twice (since the orders will exist only in the file on your hard drive).*

Using a Shopping Cart System

The most elegant and sophisticated way of setting up an online Web store is to use a shopping cart, ideally with online credit card processing. However, as mentioned earlier, this can be both complex and expensive. FrontPage has no built-in support for creating online shopping carts, so if this is a service you need, you'll have to look elsewhere. In general, there are three routes you can take.

The first route is to use one of the e-commerce companies that provide a full e-commerce solution, including all Web hosting, a shopping cart system, and credit card processing. This is definitely the easiest way to set up an online Web store, since the entire Web site is created using templates provided for you. (See Figure 7-18 for an example of a Web site created by using one of these companies.) It's also fairly inexpensive. Web sites are often provided for free, and credit card processing starts at about $25 per month, with a charge of 2.35 percent plus 20 cents per transaction. The biggest downside is the inability to create or edit your Web pages with FrontPage or any other Web page editor. This can make it difficult to implement the features and layouts you want for your Web site, and it can also result in your site appearing less than unique. Bigstep.com, Freemerchant.com, Store.Yahoo.com, and Jumbostore.com are four companies that provide these services.

Figure 7-18 An e-commerce site created on Bigstep.com.

TIP   *Many e-commerce companies offer free hosting provided that you don't require online credit card processing. If this route is appropriate for your company, consider signing up with one of the services and experimenting with their software and hosting to see whether the service is adequate for you.*

The second route that many companies take when creating an online Web store is to sign up with a Web hosting plan that includes an online shopping cart in the monthly fee. Prices vary widely, but Commerce hosting plans (or similarly named plans that provide a secure shopping cart for your Web site) can be had for as little as $30 per month. Plans often include many more features than free hosting sites, such as including support for FrontPage, more server space, and additional e-mail accounts. A Web site created using this approach is shown in Figure 7-19.

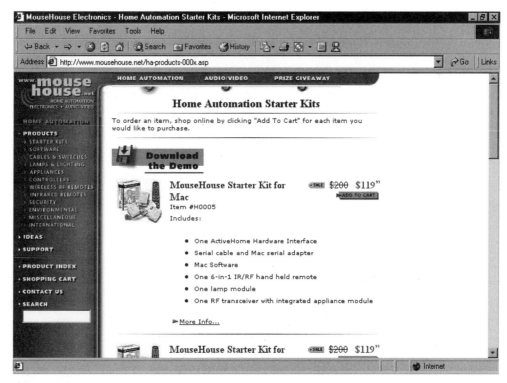

Figure 7-19 An e-commerce site that makes use of a Web hosting company's shopping cart.

This approach can be ideal for many businesses, because it allows a business to set up an online Web store—complete with online ordering for a low initial cost—and still have the flexibility to create the site using FrontPage. If you want to add online credit card processing at a later time, your Web hosting company will often provide this service for free, but with a large transaction fee (5 percent is typical); or you can get your own Internet Merchant account. However, most businesses will find it more economical to use the shopping cart to collect orders, securely connect to the Web site to view the orders that have been placed (see the previous section), and then process the orders offline using a traditional credit card reader. Forgoing online credit card processing and instead processing credit card orders using a traditional card reader usually results in lower transaction fees as well as lower monthly costs. If your online business grows enough to justify getting an Internet Merchant account, you can do so at a later time.

NOTE *Internet Merchant accounts vary in cost, but 2.39 percent plus 30 cents per transaction, with a $10 per month bank statement fee and a $25 per month monthly minimum, is an example of what to expect.*

The last method is to hire a contractor to set up your e-commerce site from scratch. This method usually yields the best results, but it is also typically very expensive. It can cost $10,000 or more depending on what features your company requires. In general, we recommend trying a more cost-effective strategy. If your needs become more sophisticated, you can always hire a contractor later, but it can be ruinous to a small company's financial state to make this kind of an expenditure on a Web site that turns out to be not as profitable as projected.

Summary

This step presented the most important ways to add interactivity to your Web site. These include creating forms to obtain information from visitors or to permit visitors to search your Web site for information, developing discussion groups on your Web site, and the options your company has for creating an online Web store. "Step 8: Deploy Your Web Site" shows you how to test your Web site for errors, publish it to the Internet, and publicize your Web site.

Step 8

DEPLOY YOUR WEB SITE

Featuring:

- Testing Your Web Site

- Publishing Your Web Site

- Publicizing Your Web Site

- Monitoring Your Web Site

After you create your Web site it's wise to perform some testing to make sure the site works properly before it's published to the Internet. When your Web site is up and running, you'll need to promote it by taking advantage of both Internet and offline advertising opportunities to generate traffic. Ongoing monitoring is a necessary part of maintaining an effective Web site, and keeping track of the number and type of visitors who come to your site as well as collecting the results of any forms are a part of this maintenance. This step demonstrates some procedures your company or organization can use to accomplish these tasks.

Testing Your Web Site

While most companies won't need to perform the exhaustive testing that large e-commerce sites must go through when rolling out a new site, a certain amount of testing before publishing your Web site can result in fewer complaints from visitors as well as a more effective site.

Here are some recommendations for Web site tests:

- Use the Reports view to check the status of your Web pages.

- Test your Web site in a variety of Web browsers to determine how well your site functions on different platforms.

- Perform usability testing with users who haven't yet seen your Web site.

TIP   *You can check for spelling errors in your entire Web site by selecting a page in the Folders view and then choosing the Tools menu's Spelling command. Select the Entire Web option, and then click Start.*

Using the Reports View to Test Your Web Site

The Reports view is one you can use to quickly find out the vital statistics of your web, and as such, it can be a valuable tool for determining whether there are any residual problems with your Web site. For example, you can assess how many broken hyperlinks are on your site, view uncompleted tasks and slow Web pages, and see a list of Web pages that won't be published to the Internet when you publish your site.

To use the Reports view, click the Reports icon on the Views bar. To view a report, double-click its name in the Site Summary list. To return to the Site Summary report after viewing a report, select Site Summary from the Report drop-down list box on the Reporting toolbar.

To run through the most important reports, follow these steps:

1. **Scan the Site Summary report.**

   The Site Summary report presents an effective overview of the current status of your FrontPage web so that you can ascertain what needs to be investigated further, as shown in Figure 8-1. Pay special attention to the following items: Slow Pages, Unverified Hyperlinks (consider verifying them), Broken Hyperlinks, Component Errors, Uncompleted Tasks.

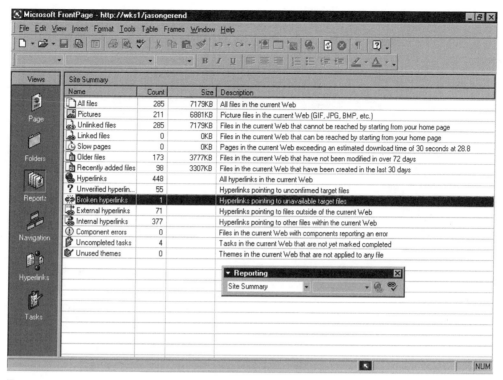

Figure 8-1 The Site Summary report in the Reports view.

2. Recalculate hyperlinks.

Choose the Tools menu's Recalculate Hyperlinks command to make sure that all hyperlink information is current. In the Recalculate Hyperlinks dialog box, click Yes to start the process, which may take several minutes.

3. Verify hyperlinks.

To check external hyperlinks for validity, click the Verify Hyperlinks button on the Reporting toolbar. In the Verify Hyperlinks dialog box that appears, click Start. (If you began hyperlink verification previously, select the Resume Verification option to start where you left off.) The Broken Hyperlinks report is displayed during and after the hyperlink verification process, as shown in Figure 8-2.

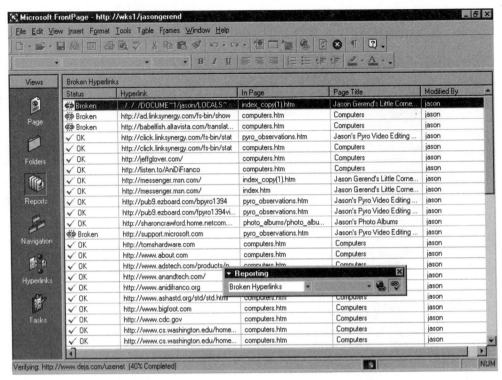

Figure 8-2   The Broken Hyperlinks report during hyperlink verification.

TIP   *To fix a hyperlink at a later time, right-click the broken hyperlink and choose Add Task from the shortcut menu to create a new task for it.*

4. Fix broken hyperlinks.

To edit a broken hyperlink, double-click it to open the Edit Hyperlink dialog box, as shown in Figure 8-3. To manually edit the hyperlink, click Edit Page. To automatically replace the hyperlink with a new or fixed hyperlink, enter the correct hyperlink in the Replace Hyperlink With box, and then click the Change In All Pages or Change In Selected Pages option button. Click Replace to implement the change.

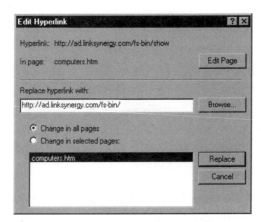

Figure 8-3   The Edit Hyperlink dialog box.

TIP   *FrontPage doesn't always recognize links properly and may incorrectly report some links as broken. If you suspect the link may be operational, verify the address in a Web browser and then manually inspect the broken link in the Web page.*

5. Check for uncompleted tasks.

In the Site Summary report, double-click the Uncompleted Tasks report (or click the Tasks icon on the Views bar). Make sure there aren't any essential tasks that need to be performed before you publish your Web site.

6. Fix any slow Web pages.

Double-click the Slow Pages report in the Site Summary report to view a list of pages that take an excessive amount of time to download (the default is 30 seconds over a 28.8 modem). Open any pages listed here, and try resizing and resampling large images or removing some images to make the pages load faster.

Testing Your Site in Different Browsers

FrontPage does a fairly accurate job of portraying your Web pages as they will appear in a Web browser, especially when viewing pages in the Preview pane (which renders the current Web page using Microsoft Internet Explorer's page rendering engine). However, your Web site might look drastically different when displayed in another company's Web browser or on a non-PC platform, such as WebTV. In order to confirm that your Web site is functional and effective for all your visitors, you need to test your site using several different browsers.

The easiest way to test your Web site in several browsers is to open each Web browser and enter the local address of your Web site in the Address or Location box, as shown in Figures 8-4, 8-5, and 8-6. For example, if your FrontPage web is named mycompany and stored on a Web server on your local network named WKS1, you would enter *http://wks1/mycompany* to open the Web site.

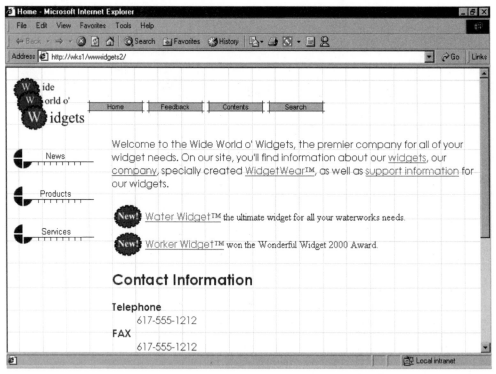

Figure 8-4   A Web site as it appears (properly) in Internet Explorer 5.

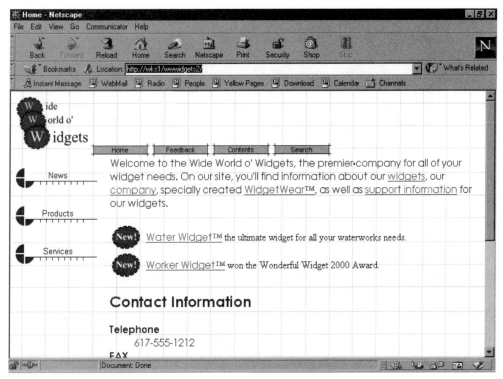

Figure 8-5   The same Web site, differing slightly in Netscape Navigator 4.7.

TIP   *If you don't know the address of your local FrontPage web, open the home page of your web in FrontPage and click the Preview In Browser toolbar button. This displays your home page, and the URL listed in the Address or Location box is the address of your local FrontPage web.*

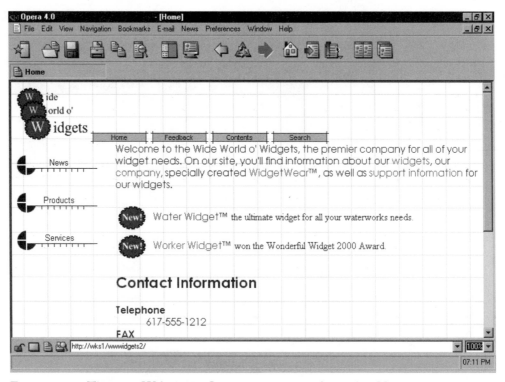

Figure 8-6 The same Web site in Opera 4, appearing identical to Netscape.

After opening your Web site in a couple of browsers, spend a few minutes testing all the links and examining each page. Is the layout consistent on all the browsers? Do all the features work as expected? Make notes on which pages have problems, and then go back into FrontPage and see whether you can fix them. (Use the Tools menu's Page Options command to change the compatibility options for FrontPage, and then modify any elements that don't display properly.)

NOTE *Test your Web site with the latest versions of Internet Explorer and Netscape Navigator. If you have access to computers running older versions of the browsers or a different browser, such as Opera, consider testing your site in these browsers, too. Testing on Macintosh and information appliances (such as WebTV) is usually easiest to do after your site has been published to the Internet.*

Usability Testing

In addition to testing for broken links and browser incompatibilities, your company or organization will find it informative to perform some degree of usability testing.

Here are some recommendations for simple usability tests:

- Recruit people who aren't involved in the Web site project to test your site. The feedback of your customers or other people in your target audience can be invaluable in evaluating the effectiveness of your site. For very small organizations, even recruiting family and friends to test your site can provide valuable feedback.

- Develop some purposeful tasks for your testers to perform, and then watch how they accomplish them. You might use tasks such as "Find the company contact information" or "Find the product information for product x." If you need to interject and help the testers, your site might need more work.

- Pay special attention to the navigational structure of your Web site. How well can users locate information using your site? See "Step 4: Collect and Organize Your Content" and "Step 6: Polish Your Pages" for more information on creating an effective navigational structure.

- Test your Web site at a variety of resolutions (see "Step 6: Polish Your Pages" for more information on creating resolution-independent Web pages). We recommend that you test your site at 640x480 (a fairly low resolution) and at 1024x768 (a typical high resolution).

- If you decide to publish your site immediately, perform the testing after it is published. A short user survey on your Web site can also be a valuable way of gathering feedback on the effectiveness of your site.

NOTE   *If your site contains online ordering capabilities, it is very important to thoroughly test your system no matter what the size of your company or Web site. For more information about online ordering, see "Step 7: Add Interactivity to Your Web Site."*

Publishing Your Web Site

When you're ready to make your Web site available to the general public on the World Wide Web, you need to publish it to the Internet.

Publishing your FrontPage web to your Web hosting company's Web server is really easy. FrontPage 2000 has built-in support for publishing both to Web servers that support FrontPage Server Extensions *and* Web servers that support publishing only via FTP. For both types of Web servers, follow these steps:

1. Click the Publish Web toolbar button.

Open the FrontPage web you want to publish to the Internet, and click the Publish Web toolbar button. This displays the Publish Web dialog box, as shown in Figure 8-7.

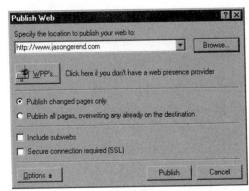

Figure 8-7   The Publish Web dialog box.

2. Enter your Web site's URL.

In the Specify The Location To Publish Your Web To box, enter the location where you want to publish your Web site (most likely your domain name, *www.mycompany.com* or perhaps *ftp://www.mycompany.com*).

3. Specify any options.

Click the Options button to display a list of available options. Click the Publish Changed Pages Only option button. If you're having trouble with certain pages, click the Publish All Pages, Overwriting Any Already On The Destination option button. If you have subwebs in your Web site, select the Include Subwebs check box to publish them along with the parent web.

4. Click Publish.

When the Name And Password Required dialog box appears, enter the name and password you use to administer your Web site (on your Web hosting company's Web server, not on your local Web server) and then click OK.

Publicizing Your Web Site

In order for your Web site to succeed, you need to publicize it. There are a number of ways to publicize your Web site, both on and off the Internet. The online methods include search engines, online advertising, newsgroups, and mailing lists. Offline methods include placing links on all print material your company or organization creates, Yellow Pages ads, and newspaper ads. These methods are discussed in greater detail in the sections that follow.

TIP   *One form of publicity that we don't cover here is word of mouth. This is not a method to underestimate. The best way to stimulate positive publicity via word of mouth is to have high-quality, timely content on your Web site.*

Submitting Your Site to Search Engines

Since most people locate a Web site using a search engine, the most important step you can take to publicize your Web site is to submit it to the top search engines. Although this process takes some time, it is very important.

TIP   *Avoid using a search engine submission service. These services usually offer to submit your site to hundreds of search engines for a sum of money—sometimes with recurring fees. Since the vast majority of searches are conducted on only a handful of search engines, this level of submission is superfluous. In addition, submission firms usually don't submit your site to directory-based search engines, or if they do, they do an inadequate job of it. Take the time to submit to search engines yourself—it's worth it.*

Before you start submitting to search engines, it helps to understand them. There are two basic types of search engines—crawler-based search engines and directories. A third type—the hybrid search engine—is a combination of the two. Crawler-based search engines automatically crawl (explore) the Web, examining Web sites and adding the relevant information from each site into their search databases. Directories such as Yahoo! take descriptions submitted by Web site authors and use human editors to review the submissions. The editors then create a hierarchical, topic-based directory out of the Web sites submitted that visitors can either browse by topic or perform a search on. Hybrid search engines are usually search engines that also contain a human-created directory. Editors create the directory by looking at the search engine's results, the actual Web sites, and sometimes sites that are submitted by site authors to the hybrid directory.

NOTE   *Web-crawling search services such as Excite can use a variety of methods to determine the content of a Web site. Most examine the home page's title, any keyword and description meta tags, as well as the text present on the home page. For information on preparing your Web site for search engines, see "Step 6: Polish Your Pages."*

NOTE   *A few search services don't fit neatly into the crawler-based, directory, or hybrid categories. For example, Ask Jeeves* (www.askjeeves.com) *uses a natural-language-processing search engine that searches a human-created database of Web sites. Mamma.com is a meta-search engine—a search engine that performs searches on a number of other search engines.*

The type of search engine determines how you'll submit your site. Crawler-based search engines generally request only your Web site's URL, as shown in Figure 8-8. The search engine then automatically visits your site, determines the content of your site, and adds it to the search engine's database.

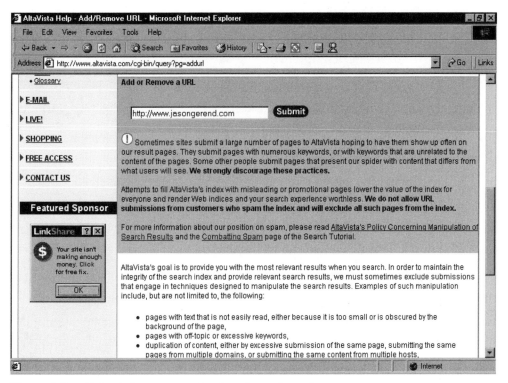

Figure 8-8   Submitting to a crawler-based search engine.

TIP   *Although search engines generally look into your Web site for what content is contained on pages other than your home page, this isn't always reliable, and it's prudent to submit your two or three most important pages separately to each search engine. (Give each of these pages a quick search engine optimization first.) But limit yourself to two or three pages; submitting too many pages to the same search engine can actually hurt your site.*

Directory-style search engines require a somewhat larger amount of effort during submission. First, visit the directory (such as Yahoo!) and perform some searches for content similar to your Web site. Second, take note of the kinds of sites that are returned in the search results and the categories under which they're listed. It's very important with directories to find the most specific and appropriate category for your Web site, so do some exploring. (Your site may belong in multiple categories. If this is the case, make a note of each one.) Third, read the directory's Site Submission Tips or the equivalent page. This will tell you exactly the procedure the directory wants you to follow when submitting your Web site. Most require that you navigate to the category under which you want to list your site, and then click the Suggest A Site link.

Fourth, in the actual submission form, as shown in Figure 8-9, submit the title of your Web site (generally your official business or company name), your site's URL, and a 25-word-or-less description of your Web site.

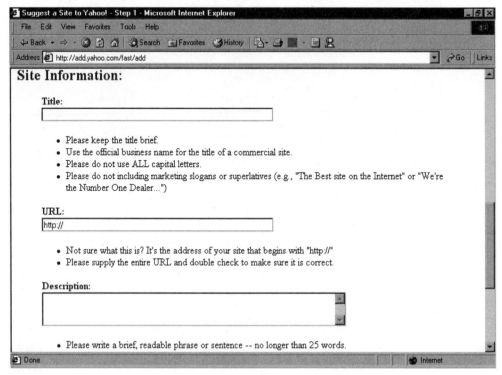

Figure 8-9 Submitting to Yahoo!'s directory.

TIP *Make your site description more than just a series of keywords. It should be a succinct, well-written summary of what visitors will find on your site.*

Table 8-1 lists search engines that we recommend you submit your site to, their URLs, and their type.

SEARCH ENGINE	URL	SEARCH ENGINE TYPE
AOL Search	search.aol.com	Hybrid using Open Directory
AltaVista	www.altavista.com	Hybrid using Open Directory and Looksmart
Direct Hit	www.directhit.com	Crawler-based, modified by popularity
Excite	www.excite.com	Crawler-based
Go/Infoseek	www.go.com	Hybrid

SEARCH ENGINE	URL	SEARCH ENGINE TYPE
Google	www.google.com	Crawler-based, modified by popularity
HotBot	www.hotbot.com and Open	Hybrid, with results from Direct Hit Directory
Looksmart	www.looksmart.com	Directory
Lycos	www.lycos.com	Hybrid, using Open Directory
MSN Search	search.msn.com	Hybrid, using Looksmart
Netscape Search	search.netscape.com	Hybrid, using Open Directory
Northern Light	www.northernlight.com	Crawler-based
Open Directory	dmoz.org	Directory
Snap	www.snap.com	Directory
WebCrawler	www.webcrawler.com	Crawler-based
Yahoo!	www.yahoo.com	Directory

Table 8-1 The major search engines.

Online Advertising

In addition to submitting your Web site to search engines, a number of other methods are available for advertising on the Web. Some of these are fairly effective in increasing the number of visitors to your Web site, and some are probably a waste of time and money. In the following sections we offer some recommendations on which methods to consider and which to ignore.

Purchasing Banner Ads

The most obvious method of online advertising is the banner ad. Banner ads are the ubiquitous (and often-ignored) rectangular ad boxes that adorn most Web sites.

In general, we recommend that you avoid paying for banner ads. They require too much time and effort to create, cost money, and are limited in their ability to draw visitors to your Web site. However, if there are any prominent Web sites that draw your target audience (such as Web sites that cover topics related to your company or organization), it may be advantageous to purchase a banner ad (although consider discussing a link exchange instead, as described below).

Link Exchanges

One of the best methods of advertising online is to get other Web sites to link to your site, creating what's known as a link exchange. This method is cost-effective (free) and can also increase your ranking in search engines that pay attention to the number of links to a particular Web site.

There are three ways that you can establish links to your company or organization's site. First, use a Link Exchange service that allows you to exchange links with other random Web sites; second, join a Web ring of sites that are similar to your own; and third, contact Web sites personally and inquire about exchanging links.

Using a Link Exchange service usually doesn't work well for most companies and organizations. This is because the Web site that ends up linking to your site usually doesn't have anything to do with your site's purpose, so it is unlikely to generate visitors who are interested in viewing your Web site. Because of this, most companies and organizations will find it more appropriate to contact relevant Web sites directly about exchanging links.

Although most link exchanges are a waste of time, Web rings devoted to a topic covered by your Web site are not. The way a Web ring works is that Web sites with a common topic contact each other, decide to set up a Web ring, and then pay to place a banner ad for the Web ring on their home pages, as shown in Figure 8-10. This banner ad is usually configured with automatically updated links to other sites in the Web ring. By joining the Web ring, your site becomes accessible through these links and is also listed in the Web ring's directory. The site *www.webring.com* is a good place to look if you are interested in joining a Web ring.

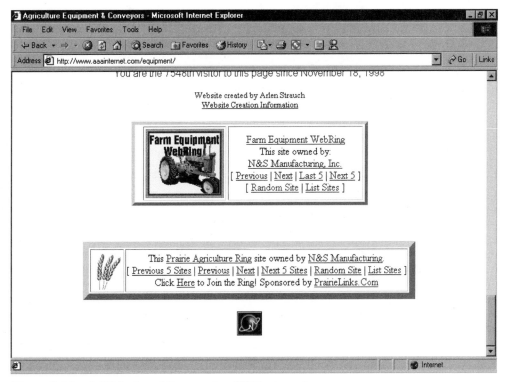

Figure 8-10   A Web site with a couple of Web ring ads.

The third method of establishing links to your Web site is to manually identify Web sites useful to your visitors with which you can exchange links. Once you've identified Web sites that cover similar or related topics, contact the sites' webmasters about setting up a link exchange.

TIP   *One way to convince a Web site to exchange links is to place a link to their site on your Web site, send them an e-mail informing them of this, and then suggest that they link to your site as well.*

Using Newsgroups to Gain Exposure

Newsgroups in general aren't the best place to publicize a Web site. Newsgroup participants usually react to ads placed on newsgroups with a fair amount of hostility, and the dynamic nature of newsgroups ensures that anything your company or organization posts will stay on the newsgroup for only a couple of weeks before getting archived or deleted.

Having said this, you can effectively use newsgroups to publicize your Web site if you're careful about how you do it. One way to publicize your Web site on a newsgroup is to locate a newsgroup that deals with issues related to your company or organization's line of business, and then post some legitimate articles on the newsgroup, such as tips or responses to questions other newsgroup members have. Along with the articles you post, make sure to include your Web site's URL, as well as a short summary of your site to entice people to visit it. Being an active and positive participant in a newsgroup can reflect well on your company or organization and also bring additional visitors to your site—just be careful to not simply post ads.

TIP   *To find a suitable newsgroup, conduct a search on Deja.com at* http://www.deja.com/usenet.

Creating a Mailing List

Mailing lists are a voluntary form of bulk e-mailing that allows a company or organization to easily send out mail, such as a newsletter or update, to a large number of people. Sending regular e-mails about your Web site or company to visitors who have joined your mailing list is an effective way of reminding visitors about your company and also featuring new or changed parts of your Web site. This increases the chances that they will visit your site again.

NOTE   *Make sure that what you send via your mailing list is valuable content to subscribers. Otherwise, your subscribers will delete the message or unsubscribe from your list. This content can include tips, how-to sections, product specials, and new additions to your Web site. Always include instructions for unsubscribing to the list with every message you send.*

You can handle mailing lists using three different types of mailing programs: a standard mail program, a stand-alone bulk mail program, or a server-based mailing list program.

TIP   *Whichever method you use to send your messages to mailing list members, consider creating a form on your Web site that visitors can use to subscribe to your mailing list. To do so, either insert the code provided to you by your mailing list provider or create a simple form with a text box for e-mail address input and a Submit button. Configure the form to send the results to either your e-mail address and/or a form results file on your Web server. See "Step 7: Add Interactivity to Your Web Site" for more information on creating forms.*

You can use a standard e-mail program, such as Microsoft Outlook or Outlook Express, to send mail to everyone on your list, provided the number of subscribers is small. To use Outlook or Outlook Express, create a separate folder in your Contacts folder or Address Book for the mailing list subscribers, create a contact for each subscriber, and then add each user to the BCC field of a new mail message. This method is inconvenient and slow, but it is relatively simple to set up and it can work well for a beginning mailing list. Most companies and organizations will find themselves quickly outgrowing it, however.

Another method is to use a stand-alone bulk mailer program, such as Aureate Group Mail *(http://www.group-mail.com)*. Bulk mail programs are specially designed for sending out an e-mail message to a large number of mailing list subscribers. These programs are generally inexpensive ($50 is a typical price) and are an appropriate option for companies or organizations that don't require the sophistication of a server-based mailing list solution (as described below).

The most sophisticated and complicated method of creating a mailing list is to use a server-based mailing list program, such as L-Soft's Listserv *(www.lsoft.com)* or Majordomo. Both of these programs are typically provided to you by your Web hosting company for an additional monthly fee—starting at roughly $15 per month for a small number of subscribers. One advantage of using a server-based solution is the ability to allow users to subscribe and unsubscribe from the mailing list themselves, although this advantage is somewhat offset by the difficulty of configuring and maintaining the mailing list. If your company or organization finds itself outgrowing bulk mail programs though, a server-based mail program can be an excellent solution.

TIP   *Many companies and organizations will find that Web-based mailing list providers such as eGroups.com and Listbot (www.listbot.com) are a better solution than the traditional Listserv and Majordomo programs. Additionally, many of these Web-based list servers can be used for free, provided you don't mind having ads inserted in your messages.*

Offline Publicizing

Your company or organization can get so caught up in publicizing your Web site online that you forget about the more traditional channels of publicity, such as company publications, phone books, and newspaper ads, and traditional marketing methods, such as speaking engagements.

Any time that you draw attention to your business or organization, you'll increase the number of visitors to your Web site—provided that you make it clear to your audience how to find your Web site. Generally, you publicize your Web site in the same way that you would publicize your company, but in addition to (or possibly instead of) providing a phone number as a contact method, list your URL. Many people consider the Web their preferred source of information, so any time you want to provide people with a way of obtaining additional information about your company or organization, list your URL.

Here are some recommendations for offline channels that you may want to consider for publicizing your Web site:

- Company letterhead. Include your URL in your letterhead design.

- Business cards, magnets, and stickers. Print the company URL on all employee business cards, as well as magnets, stickers, and any other ephemera your company prints.

- Print newsletters or other documents. Include your Web site's URL prominently in any print newsletters or flyers your company or organization creates, and consider including a small summary or highlights of the information contained on your site.

- Answering machine or voice mail. Tell callers about additional information that can be obtained from your Web site, and provide the URL.

- Phone books and newspaper ads. Revise your Yellow Pages listing to include your URL, and make sure to print your URL in any newspaper or other print ads you run.

- Speaking engagements and broadcast media. Mention your Web site address during a media appearance, but keep the references short, professional, and low-key.

Monitoring Your Web Site

After you publish and publicize your Web site, it's important to monitor your site for new form results, as well as to determine the number of visitors who come to your site and the type of browsers they are using. This can give you a better feel for whether or not your Web site is achieving its desired results, demonstrate the effectiveness of your Web site publicity efforts, and perhaps reveal whether or not you need to rethink the browser compatibility of your Web site.

FrontPage by default stores form results in the _private directory of your Web site, making them inaccessible except directly through FrontPage. In order to download or view the form results, you need to open your Internet Web site directly in FrontPage instead of opening the local copy of your Web site, as you would normally do. To do this, choose the File menu's Open Web command, enter your Web site's address in the Folder Name box, and then click Open. Enter the username and password for the Web site, and then locate the form results in the _private directory.

To obtain useful statistics on your Web site's usage patterns, such as the number of visitors coming to your site or what browsers they're using, you need to use a third-party monitoring solution. Typically, your Web hosting company will provide usage statistics for your site as a part of your Web hosting package, as shown in Figure 8-11. However, if this service isn't included with your hosting plan, or if the statistics provided are inadequate, you can use a third party to collect statistics on your Web site traffic. Some companies that offer Web site statistics collection include Counter.com, Sitegauge.com, and Fxweb.com/tracker.

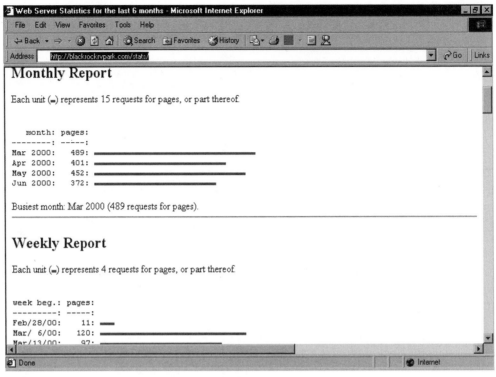

Figure 8-11   The traffic statistics for a Web site.

Here are some recommendations about what to look for when reading the statistics for your Web site:

- Total number of visits and average hits per day. This number tells you how many people are visiting your Web site, although it may include multiple visits by the same person.

- How visitors are finding your site. Some usage statistics show which Web sites referred visitors to your site. This can be invaluable for determining your most important referral sources.

- What type of Web browsers visitors are using to view your site. Seeing the break-down of which browsers and browser versions are being used to view your site helps you better tailor your Web site to your visitors.

- What type of operating systems are being used to view your site. This information can help identify the platforms on which you should test your Web site, as well as show you how up-to-date your visitors are.

Summary

In this last step, we showed you how to test your site for errors or design problems, as well as publish the site to your Web hosting company's Internet Web server. We also gave you some strategies and suggestions for publicizing your Web site, both online and offline, as well as briefly discussing components to monitor on your Web site after it's published. In the Appendix "Set Up Your Web Site on a Local Web Server," we discuss setting up your FrontPage web on a local Windows 2000 Web server.

Appendix

SET UP YOUR WEB SITE ON A LOCAL WEB SERVER

Featuring:

- Why Use a Local Web Server?

- Configuring Internet Information Server

In addition to creating a central content folder (discussed in "Step 4: Collect and Organize Your Content"), it's a good practice to set up a folder to contain the local copy of your Web site—that is, the location where your Web site is stored before it's uploaded to your Web server. This can be any folder on any machine, but to thoroughly test your Web site, it should be located on a computer on your network that is running Web server software, such as Microsoft Internet Information Server (IIS), which is included with Windows NT and Windows 2000.

Why Use a Local Web Server?

Here are some of the advantages of storing the local copy of your Web site (which FrontPage calls a FrontPage web) on a Web server:

- User feedback forms and search forms can be tested before you publish the site to the Internet.

- Discussion pages can be tested.

- Database interactions can be tested.

- Security can be implemented locally on your Web site, allowing you to control who can edit pages on your Web site.

Configuring Internet Information Server

Setting up a Web server and creating a new directory on it for your Web site can be a little daunting. If you have someone in your company or organization who handles configuring your computers, have that person do this for you. However, the process itself isn't really that difficult, especially if you're running Windows 2000.

If IIS is already configured and running on a local computer, you can easily create the folder right at the time you create your Web site in FrontPage, so skip the rest of this Appendix (unless you want to test search forms, in which case, go to step 10 below).

NOTE   *IIS doesn't run on Windows 98, although you can use Personal Web Server, a limited Web server that is available for use on Windows 98. However, Personal Web Server doesn't provide the enhanced FrontPage support that IIS does, making it only moderately useful for testing your Web site.*

If you don't have a Web server configured, use the brief description that follows. (The following procedure describes the setup for Windows 2000; it will be slightly different for Windows NT 4.) To configure a server, follow these steps:

1. **Make sure IIS is installed.**

   If any computers on your local network are running Windows 2000 with IIS installed, use one of those computers. Otherwise, on a Windows 2000 computer, click the Start button, choose Settings and then click Control Panel. Double-click Add/Remove Programs, click Add/Remove Windows Components, select Indexing Service (if not already selected and you want to test Web site search forms), and then select Internet Information Services (IIS), as shown in Figure A-1. Click Next to perform the installation.

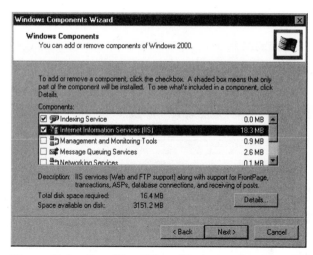

Figure A-1   Installing IIS and Indexing Service in Windows 2000.

2. Create a new folder for your Web site.

Your FrontPage web needs to be stored somewhere. You can use any directory to store the local version of your Web site, although it's usually placed either in the \Inetpub folder on your local Web server in a subdirectory named after your Web site (for example, \Inetpub\mycompany) or in a folder near your central content folder. This folder doesn't have to be located on the local Web server; it can be on any accessible computer on your local network, as long as you create a virtual directory for it, as described below. In any case, create the folder using the same procedure described in the "Creating a Central Content Location" section in "Step 4: Collect and Organize Your Content."

NOTE   *The \Inetpub folder is the default location for Web sites in IIS, and it is usually located on the drive on which Windows 2000 or Windows NT is stored.*

TIP   *If you want to control who in your company or organization can access and edit pages on your Web site, it's best to create the folder on a drive using the NTFS file system, which provides advanced security features.*

3. Open the Computer Management tool.

From the Control Panel folder of your local Web server, double-click the Administrative Tools folder, and then double-click the Computer Management tool to open it. Click the plus sign next to Services And Applications, and then click the plus sign next to Internet Information Services to view your local Web server's properties.

4. Start the Virtual Directory Creation Wizard.

Right-click Default Web Site listed under Internet Information Services, as shown in Figure A-2. Choose New from the shortcut menu, and choose Virtual Directory from the submenu to start the Virtual Directory Creation Wizard.

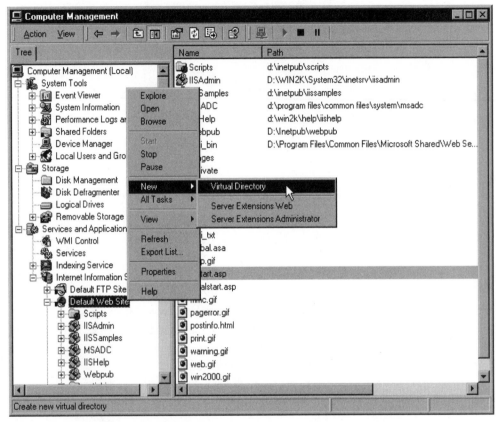

Figure A-2   Starting IIS's Virtual Directory Creation Wizard in Windows 2000.

5. Enter an alias for your local Web site.

Click Next in the first screen of the wizard, and then enter in the Alias box the name you want to use to access your Web site locally. For example, if the domain name for your Web site is *www.mycompany.com,* consider using *mycompany* as the alias. Click Next.

6. Specify in which directory your Web site will be located.

In the Directory box, enter the path to the folder where your Web site will be stored. Click Browse to visually locate the directory, if that's easier, and then click Next.

7. **Enter the username and password required for the folder.**

   If the folder that will store your FrontPage web is located on a network disk instead of locally on the Web server, enter the username and password of a user with Administrator privileges for that network disk. Click Next.

8. **Specify the permissions for the folder.**

   Select the Read, Run Scripts, Write, and Browse permissions to allow you to properly create, administer, and test your Web site locally before publishing it to your Internet Web server. Click Next, and then click Finish to complete the wizard. Your FrontPage web can now be created, accessed, and tested on your local Web server.

9. **Configure FrontPage Server Extensions for the web.**

   In order to use the new Web site in FrontPage, right-click the directory under Default Web Site, choose All Tasks from the shortcut menu, and choose Configure Server Extensions from the submenu. Click Next in each screen of the New Subweb Wizard to use the default settings, and then click Finish.

   TIP   *If the folder you created was previously a FrontPage web, right-click the virtual directory you created under Default Web Site, choose All Tasks from the shortcut menu, and then choose Check Server Extensions from the submenu.*

10. **Turn on the Indexing Service to permit testing search forms.**

    If you want to be able to test any search forms you create for your Web site (as discussed in "Step 7: Add Interactivity to Your Web Site"), you need to turn on Windows 2000's Indexing Service, if it's not already enabled. To do this, right-click the Indexing Service icon immediately above the Internet Information Services icon in Computer Management, and choose Start from the shortcut menu. Click Yes when asked whether you want to run the Indexing Service automatically when you start your computer. Otherwise, your search forms will work only until the computer is rebooted.

GLOSSARY

Active Server Pages

Abbreviated ASP. Dynamically created pages from a Microsoft Access or SQL database.

Banner ad

A rectangular-shaped advertisement on a Web page.

Bookmark

A placeholder within a Web page that allows **hyperlinks** to refer to this location within the Web page.

Cable modem

A device that allows computers to access the **Internet** using a cable TV connection. The local cable TV company must enable cable modem access to a home or business in order for a cable **modem** to work.

Cascading Style Sheets

Abbreviated CSS. A standard for applying formatting and positioning information to a Web page. CSS information can be used within a Web page or placed in an external style sheet file. Web pages that are linked to external style sheets obtain text formatting information from the style sheet (an excellent way to standardize the look for many pages in a **Web site**).

Chat

A form of real-time communication that typically involves two or more users typing messages to each other.

CGI Scripts

A standard for running small programs on a **Web server.** Typically used on Unix Web servers.

Content folder

A separate folder in which to store content before it is added to a **Web site.**

Crawler-based search engine

A **search engine** that automatically "crawls" the Web searching for **Web sites** to examine and include in the search engine's database of Web sites.

Discussion group

A part of a **Web site** that emulates **newsgroups,** allowing visitors to post messages and read and reply to other visitors' messages.

Domain

A group of computers on a network that all use a central server to handle users and security policies. The server must run either Windows NT Server or Windows 2000 Server.

Domain name

The main part of a Web address. Domain names usually represent companies, organizations, or individuals and must be registered with an accredited domain name **registrar.**

DNS

An abbreviation for Domain Name Service. Translates numerical IP addresses into user- friendly **domain names,** and vice versa.

DSL

An abbreviation for Digital Subscriber Line. A persistent (always on) high-speed form of **Internet** access that works over standard telephone lines that qualify for DSL service.

E-mail

A form of communication that involves sending mail-like messages across a network (typically the **Internet**).

E-mail account

An **e-mail** address that has its own mailbox, that is, mail isn't forwarded to another account as is the case with **E-mail aliases.**

E-mail alias

An e-mail alias works like a sort of virtual **e-mail** address that forwards received mail to another address.

Encryption

The process of scrambling data to prevent unauthorized users from viewing the data.

Form handler

The software that gathers data from a form. Form handlers are either a part of FrontPage Server Extensions or CGI scripts.

Frames

An **HTML** feature that permits splitting a Web page into multiple areas (frames) within which separate Web pages are displayed. Not supported by all **Web browsers.**

FrontPage Server Extensions

A set of extensions to **Web servers** that FrontPage uses to easily accomplish advanced server-based tasks, such as handling submitted form data.

FrontPage web

A Web site that is created with FrontPage. Typically, once a web is published to the **Internet** it is referred to as a Web site.

GIF

An abbreviation for Graphics Interchange Format. A file format used most commonly for small graphics on Web pages. Contains a maximum of 256 colors and can be made partially transparent or into a short animation.

Home page

Also called a front page. The first page that is displayed on a **Web site,** typically named index.html, index.htm, or Default.htm.

Host name

The name of an individual computer on the **Internet** or **intranet.** It is the leftmost part of a Web address. For example, for the address *wks1.microsoft.com,* the host name is *wks1.*

HTML

An abbreviation for Hypertext Markup Language. The coding language used to create Web pages.

Hyperlink

A piece of text or image that when clicked takes the visitor to another page, image, or file.

IIS

An abbreviation for Internet Information Server. A Microsoft **Web server** program that comes with Windows NT and Windows 2000.

Instant Messaging

A form of communication that is roughly a cross between **chat** and telephone. Users run an Instant Messaging program that notifies them when people they know are online. Users can then conduct a text-based "conversation."

Internet

A worldwide computer network running the TCP/IP protocol suite and consisting of hundreds of millions of computers.

Intranet

A private network that uses **Internet** technology - the TCP/IP protocol suite and **Web servers.**

Internet Merchant Account

An account with a bank or financial institution for the purpose of processing online credit card transactions.

Internet service provider

Abbreviated ISP. A company that provides access to the **Internet** via dial-up connections, **DSL**, leased lines, or other connection methods.

IP address

The unique address for a single network card on a network using TCP/IP. All computers (hosts) on the Internet or an **intranet** must have an IP address to communicate.

ISDN

An abbreviation for Integrated Services Digital Network. A form of moderately high-speed **Internet** connection, ISDN uses one or two telephone lines that are configured for ISDN service and provides a typical maximum of 128Kbps when both lines are used.

JPEG

An abbreviation for Joint Photographic Experts Group. A file format used for photos and other high-quality images on Web pages. Uses image compression to reduce file size.

Keyword

A word placed in a Web page using a **meta tag** to allow **search engines** to recognize that the Web page contains content related to the keyword.

Local Area Network

Abbreviated LAN. A group of computers that are all located within the same local area (typically one building) and that can communicate with each other.

Mailing list

A list to which users can subscribe that allows them to receive **e-mail** messages on a particular topic sent by a company or organization.

Meta tags

Also known as meta variables. Meta tags store information about a **Web site,** such as a description and **keywords. Crawler-based search engines** often use these tags to determine when to display your Web site in a list of search results, as well as what description to display.

Modem

An analog device that allows a computer to communicate with other computers over standard telephone lines. Capable of a maximum of 53Kbps download rate.

Multiprocessing

Using more than one processor in a single computer. Each processor can work independently, making multiprocessing-aware applications faster.

Navigation bars

A series of buttons or **hyperlinks** that help visitors quickly access the most important pages on a **Web site.**

Newsgroups

Electronic bulletin boards on the **Internet** where people can post messages, read other users' posts, and reply to them.

Page banner

An automatically created heading that displays the title of the Web page.

Permissions

The level of access given to a user or group for a particular file or folder.

PNG

An abbreviation for Portable Network Graphic. A newer file format designed for high-quality images with optional transparency. Not supported by all **Web browsers.**

RAID

An abbreviation for Redundant Array of Inexpensive Disks. A collection of hard drives that is treated as one drive by the operating system and usually provides extra speed and reliability.

Registrar

A company that is permitted to sell Internet **domain names.**

Resample

To change the amount of information stored in a file. Images that are reduced in size using FrontPage should be resampled to improve image quality and reduce image size.

Search engine

A program contained on a **Web site** that allows visitors to search for Web pages on the **Internet.**

Shared border

A border that FrontPage creates along one edge (typically) of all Web pages in your **Web site.** This is an ideal place to put **navigation bars,** page titles, copyright information, and other information you might want to place in a header or footer.

SSL

An abbreviation for Secure Sockets Layer. A way of **encrypting** data that is transferred to and from a **Web site** and is typically used for **Web stores** that process credit card transactions.

Subdomain

A **domain** that is a child of another domain. For example, *support.microsoft.com* is a subdomain of *microsoft.com.*

Table

A formatting tool that enables text and images to be placed in a grid. Tables are extremely useful for creating advanced layouts on Web pages.

Tag

The building block of an **HTML** document. It begins with a < and ends with an >.

Template

A Web page that acts as a starting point for new Web pages. Any content or formatting information on a template is automatically applied to new pages created with the template, streamlining the creation of some Web pages.

Theme

Groups of colors, graphics, and fonts that you can apply to individual Web pages or an entire **FrontPage web.**

Thumbnail image

A small version of an image that is **hyperlinked** to the full-size version.

Top-level domain

The highest level (rightmost) part of a **domain name,** for example, .com, .net, or .org.

Underscore

The "_" character. It is often used to represent a space in filenames on the **Internet** because it is compatible with both the Windows naming scheme and the Unix naming scheme.

UPS

An abbreviation for Uninterruptible Power Supply. A battery backup for a computer, or occasionally, a backup generator that ensures that a computer can continue operating, or at least shut down properly, in the event of a power failure.

URL

An abbreviation for Uniform Resource Locator. An address for a file, usually on the **Internet.**

Views

Different ways of displaying your **FrontPage web** and its Web pages. View options are available on the Views bar.

Virtual domains

The ability to make a single computer host multiple **domain names**. When discussing **Web hosting** plans, virtual domain support means that you can use your own **domain name**.

Web browser

A program used to display Web pages.

Web hosting

To store a **Web site** and make it available for others to view on the **Internet**.

Web ring

A collection of **Web sites** that all cover the same topic and that post a Web ring **banner ad** on their sites allowing visitors to easily view other sites in the Web ring.

Web server

A computer that is running a Web server program, enabling it to serve Web pages to other hosts on the **Internet** or a **LAN**.

Web site

A collection of interlinked Web pages, usually pertaining to the same general topic or created by the same company, organization, individual, or group.

Web store

A **Web site** which visitors can browse and then purchase products or services.

Workgroup

A group of people who work together. Alternatively, a network that doesn't use a **domain** controller—also called a peer-to-peer network .

Index

majordomos
   for creating mailing lists, 211
   Web host support for, 50–51
Mamma.com Web site, 204
MB (megabytes), 2
.mcw files, 76
megabytes, 2
menu bar, FrontPage, 104
meta tags, 11, 147
Microsoft FrontPage. *See* FrontPage 2000
Microsoft Knowledge Base, 31–32
Microsoft Locate A Web Presence Provider Web
   site, 55–56
Microsoft Product Support Services Web site, 32
Microsoft WebTV, 150
.mid files, 77
modems, 2, 3, 4
moving files between folders, 105, 115
MSN Search, 207

naming files, 68-69, 119
navigating Web sites, 16
navigation bars, 107, 108, 143–44
Navigation toolbar, 107, 108
Navigation view, 107–8
Netscape Navigator, 114, 199, 200. *See also* Web
   browsers
Netscape Search, 207
.net top-level domain, 44
Network Solutions, 47, 59
new folders, creating, 66-68
newsgroups, 7, 210
new Web sites, creating, 96–102
Normal tab, Page view, 111–12
Northern Light search engine, 207
numbered lists, 121

O

OCR programs, 90
offline advertising, 212
online catalogs, 21–23, 183, 184, 186, 188

online discussion groups
   chat-based, 33–34, 178
   creating, 178–82
   overview, 32–33, 177, 178
online photo services, 88-89
online shopping carts, 189–92
Open Directory search engine, 207
opening
   Web pages, 102–3
   webs, 102–3
Opera browser, 198, 200
ordering information, 22–23
.org top-level domain, 44
.otm files, 76

P

Page Banners feature, 145
Page Properties dialog box, 156
pages. *See* Web pages
Page view
   HTML tab, 112–13
   Normal tab, 111–12
   overview, 105, 111
   Preview tab, 113–14
paragraphs
   aligning, 121
   as bulleted lists, 121
   formatting, 120–21
   indenting, 121
   as numbered lists, 121
passwords, 59–60, 203
.pcd files, 77
.pcx files, 77
permissions, 132–35
photos. *See also* images
   from digital cameras, 82-83
   and online photo services, 88-89
   and picture CDs, 85-88
   scanning, 81, 82, 83-84
   transmission times, 3–4
PhotoWorks.com Web site, 88

T

T1 connections, 52–53
tables. *See also* cells, table
    adding, 159–61
    adding background images, 163
    adding content, 161
    aligning cell contents, 163
    changing alignment, 162
    changing background, 163
    changing border colors, 163
    changing border thickness, 163
    changing cell spacing, 162
    changing properties, 161–63
    changing table height, 162
    changing table width, 162
    coloring background, 163
    coloring borders, 163
    creating, 159–61
    drawing, 160–61
    inserting, 159–60
    overview, 158–59
    resizing, 162, 163
    specifying size, 162–63
    wrapping text around, 162
tags, HTML, 9–11
tasks
    adding to Tasks view, 110
    assigning, 137
    deleting, 111
    editing, 111
    marking completed, 111
    uncompleted, 197
    viewing, 137
Tasks view, 109–11
telephones, communicating via Internet, 8
templates
    creating from existing Web pages, 154–55
    for creating Web pages, 117
    for creating Web sites, 97
    saving Web pages as, 154–55
    vs. wizards, 97

testing
    hyperlinks, 194–97
    search forms, 177
    usability, 201
    Web sites, 193–201
text
    adding hyperlinks, 121–22
    aligning, 121, 125–26
    boldfacing, 121
    entering, 120–21
    formatting, 120–21
    highlighting, 121
    importing, 119–20
    indenting, 121
    italicizing, 121
    specifying font, 121
    spell checking, 120
    underlining, 121
    wrapping, 162
text boxes, 171, 172, 173
.tga files, 77
themes
    applying to Web pages or sites, 157–58
    choosing in Web wizards, 101–2
thumbnails, 80, 127
.tiff files, 76
.tif files, 76
titles, Web page, 117
<title> tag, 11
to-do list. *See* tasks
toolbars, FrontPage, 104
top-level domains, 41–42, 44
transaction processing, as reason to have Web site, 13–14
transparent images, 79, 124
.txt files, 76

U

Under Construction icon, 101
underlining text, 121
UPS Web site, 23
URLs, how they work, 6, 10–11, 122
U.S. Internal Revenue Service Web site, 23–24
usability testing, 201
usernames, setting up, 129–30
users
    adding to groups, 135
    creating, 130
    deleting, 130
    removing from groups, 135
    specifying permissions, 135

V

verifying hyperlinks, 195
Views bar, 104, 105
Virtual Directory Creation Wizard, 220–21
virtual domains, defined, 48

W

.wav files, 77
Web. *See* FrontPage webs; Web pages; Web sites; World Wide Web
Web-based storefronts, 182–92
Web browsers
    making Web pages compatible with, 148–50
    previewing Web pages, 113–14
    role of, 6
    testing Web sites in, 197–200
WebCrawler, 207
Web hosting companies
    Active Server Pages support, 49
    assessing Web server reliability, 53–54
    assessing Web server speed, 52–53
    choosing, 47–55
    comparing features, 48–54
    database support, 49
    data transfer limitations, 51

disk space allotment, 48–49
    domain hosting support, 48
    and domain names, 47, 58–59
    e-mail accounts, 49–50
    local vs. national, 54
    mailing list support, 50–51
    shopping cart services, 190–91
    signing up for service, 57–62
    and SSL security, 51
    subdomain support, 50
    support for FrontPage 2000 Server Extensions, 48, 54
    technical support, 51–52
    virtual domain support, 48
    where to find, 55–57
Web pages. *See also* content, Web site; Web sites
    adding bookmarks to, 123
    adding images, 123
    adding page banners, 145
    adding to webs, 115
    changing background, 155–56
    changing colors, 155–56
    checking hyperlinks, 194–97
    checking in and out, 131–32, 136
    closing, 103
    creating, 116–17
    creating consistent look and feel, 153–64
    creating headings, 120–21
    creating hyperlinks, 121–23
    creating site plan for, 92–94
    defined, 6
    editing hyperlinks, 196
    entering text, 120–21
    entering URLs, 122
    exporting, 119
    formatting text, 120–21
    how they work, 9
    importing, 115
    inserting text into, 119–20
    making compatible with multiple browsers, 148–50
    opening, 102–3
    previewing in Internet Explorer, 113–14

X

.xls files, 76
.xlw files, 76
XML, 12

Y

Yahoo! Web site, 26, 203, 207

The manuscript for this book was prepared and submitted to Redmond Technology Press in electronic form. Text files were prepared using Microsoft Word 2000. Pages were composed using PageMaker 6.5 for Windows, with text in Frutiger and Caslon. Composed files were delivered to the printer as electronic prepress files.

Interior Design

Stefan Knorr

Project Editor

Paula Thurman

Technical Editor

Anne Sandbo

Indexer

Julie Kawabata

Layout

Janaya Carter

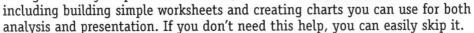
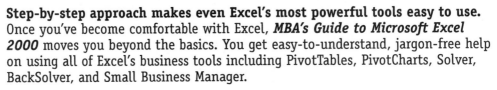

ARE YOU AN EXECUTIVE USER OF THE INTERNET WHO NEEDS TO GET STARTED QUICKLY?

Written specifically for busy executives, managers, and other professionals, *Effective Executive's Guide to the Internet* provides a fast-paced, executive summary of the seven core skills you need to know to use the Internet at work, on the road, or at home:

Skill 1: Understanding the Environment. This skill gives you an overview of the Internet: what it is, how it works, and how it came to be.

Skill 2: Making Internet Connections. This skill provides step-by-step instructions for connecting your computer or network to the Internet.

Skill 3: Browsing the Web. This skill focuses on the Internet Explorer Web browser included with all the latest versions of Windows. We explain how a Web browser works and how to customize Internet Explorer.

Skill 4: Communicating with Electronic Mail. In this skill, we describe how to use Outlook Express, the mail and news reader included with Windows.

Skill 5: Using Search Services. This skill describes in detail how search services work and you can best use them. A special topic at the end of this skill gives you some ways to get started gathering business information.

Skill 6: Understanding Other Internet Services. In this skill, we look at FTP, Telnet, Mailing lists, and using your computer as a fax machine and telephone.

Skill 7: Publishing on the Web. Learn how Web pages work, how to develop a Web strategy, how to set up your domain and your server, how to collect and create digital content, and how to create your Web page.

ABOUT THE AUTHORS:

Pat Coleman writes about intranets, the Internet, and Microsoft Windows 2000. Formerly the editorial director of Microsoft Press, Coleman is also the co-author of the best-selling *Effective Executive's Guide to Project 2000* and *Effective Executive's Guide to Windows 2000,* both published by Redmond Technology Press.

Stephen L. Nelson: With more than 3 million books sold in English, Nelson is arguably the best-selling author writing about using computers in business. Formerly a senior consultant with Arthur Andersen & Co., he is also the co-author of *Effective Executive's Guide to Project 2000* and *Effective Executive's Guide to PowerPoint 2000.*

288 pages, paperback, $24.95   Available at bookstores everywhere and at all online bookstores.
ISBN 0-9672981-0-5

DO YOU NEED TO GET YOUR PROJECT STARTED QUICKLY?

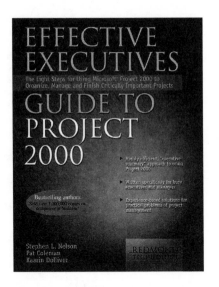

Written specifically for busy executives and project managers, *Effective Executives— Guide to Project 2000* walks you through the eight steps of organizing, managing and finishing your project using Microsoft® Project 2000:

Step 1: Learn the Language. Start here with a refresher on the language of project management and Project 2000.

Step 2: Describe the Project. Describe your project in general terms, including start date, end date and calendar of workdays.

Step 3: Schedule Project Tasks. Break your project down into component tasks, specifying task order and relationships.

Step 4: Identify and Assign Project Resources. Identify and then allocate project resources, such as people and equipment.

Step 5: Review Project Organization. Review your project for structural soundness and reasonableness.

Step 6: Present Project to Stakeholders. Present your plan to project team members and management.

Step 7: Manage Project Progress. Monitor progress and costs, assuring your project stays on course.

Step 8: Communicate Project Status. As the project progresses, keep project team members and other stakeholders apprised of the project's status and communicate important project information and changes.

ABOUT THE AUTHORS:

With more than 3,000,000 books sold in English, **Stephen L. Nelson** is arguably the best-selling author writing about using computers in business. Nelson's project management experience includes work in software development, commercial real estate development and book publishing.

Pat Coleman is a technical editor and author who writes about intranets, the Internet, Windows, and Windows applications. The co-author of *Mastering Intranets, Mastering Internet Explorer 4,* and *Windows 2000 Professional: In Record Time* (all published by SYBEX), Coleman has worked as the editorial director of Microsoft Press, deputy editor at World Almanac and as a project analyst at Encyclopaedia Britannica.

Kaarin Dolliver is the managing editor of Redmond Technology Press and has been a contributing editor to a series of bestselling books.

304 pages, paperback, $24.95   Available at bookstores everywhere and at all online bookstores
ISBN: 0-9672981-1-3

DO YOU WANT TO GET A DREAMWEAVER WEB SITE UP AND RUNNING QUICKLY?

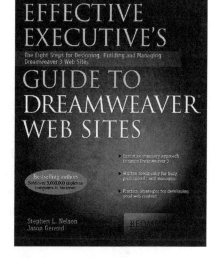

Written specifically for busy executives, managers, and other professionals, *Effective Executive's Guide to Dreamweaver Web Sites* walks you through the eight steps of designing, building, and managing Dreamweaver 3 Web sites:

Step 1: Learn the Logic. Start here with a discussion about how the Web works, why Web sites make sense, and what makes a site effective.

Step 2: Develop a Content Strategy. Identify the purpose of the Web site and the required content.

Step 3: Lay a Foundation. Prepare the foundation of your Web site by getting a domain name and locating a company to host your Web site.

Step 4: Collect and Organize Your Content. Collect existing content or develop new content—then create a central warehouse to store and organize this material.

Step 5: Create Your Web Site. Set up your Web pages and other Web site components using Dreamweaver.

Step 6: Polish Your Pages. Refine your Web pages to make them more effective and professional.

Step 7: Add Interactivity to Your Web Site. Enhance your Web site through the addition of interactive features.

Step 8: Deploy Your Web Site. Test and publish your Web site and then draw attention to it by submitting your site to search engines, sharing links, using newsgroups and list servers, and generating offline publicity.

More than just a book about Dreamweaver, *Effective Executive's Guide to Dreamweaver Web Sites* explains how to create business and nonprofit organization Web sites that really work.

ABOUT THE AUTHORS:

Stephen L. Nelson: With more than 3 million books sold in English, Nelson is arguably the best-selling author writing about using computers in business. Formerly a senior consultant with Arthur Andersen & Co., he is also the co-author of *Effective Executive's Guide to Project 2000* (Redmond Technology Press 2000).

Jason Gerend: Gerend, a freelance technical writer, has contributed to or co-authored a series of acclaimed and best-selling computer books, including *Effective Executive's Guide to FrontPage Web Sites* (Redmond Technology Press 2000).

304 pages, paperback, $24.95   Available at bookstores everywhere and at all online bookstores
ISBN: 0-9672981-9-9

ARE YOU AN EXECUTIVE USER OF WINDOWS 2000 PROFESSIONAL?

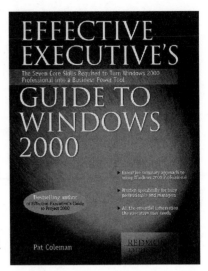

Written specifically for busy executives, managers, and other professionals, *Effective Executive's Guide to Windows 2000* provides a fast-paced, filtered executive summary of the seven core skills you need to know to use Microsoft Windows 2000 Professional at work, on the road, or even at home:

> **Skill 1: Understanding the Desktop.** This skill explains logging on, using the Start menu, using the Taskbar, working with the desktop icons, and creating shortcuts.

Skill 2: Managing Files and Folders. This skill explains the Windows 2000 Professional file systems, including how to organize and protect your documents.

Skill 3: Printing. This skill shows you how to install and manage a local printer, how to print documents, how to customize the printing process, and how to install and use fonts.

Skill 4: Working on a Network. This skill gives you step-by-step instructions for setting up a small network, installing a network printer, setting up users and groups, and installing network applications.

Skill 5: Customizing Windows 2000 Professional. This skill suggests ways to customize everything from the display to the hardware.

Skill 6: Using the Internet. This skill tells you how to connect to the Internet and how to use Internet Explorer and Outlook Express.

Skill 7: Preventive Maintenance and Troubleshooting. This skill gives you guidelines for protecting the health of your computer, maintaining the system, and troubleshooting when a problem arises.

In addition, *Effective Executive's Guide to Windows 2000* also includes two appendixes that review the Windows 2000 Professional Accessories (including Address Book, NetMeeting, Notepad, WordPad, Fax Service, and Calculator) and explain how to use Windows 2000 Professional on a portable computer.

ABOUT THE AUTHOR:

Pat Coleman is a technical editor and author who writes about intranets, the Internet, and Microsoft Windows 2000. Coleman is also the co-author of the best-selling *Effective Executive's Guide to Project 2000* and *Effective Executive's Guide to the Internet,* both published by Redmond Technology Press.

304 pages, paperback, $24.95   Available at bookstores everywhere and at all online bookstores
ISBN: 0-9672981-8-0